The U.S. Economy

Jill Hamilton, *Book Editor*

GREENHAVEN PRESS
A part of Gale, Cengage Learning

Detroit • New York • San Francisco • New Haven, Conn • Waterville, Maine • London

GALE
CENGAGE Learning™

Christine Nasso, *Publisher*
Elizabeth Des Chenes, *Managing Editor*

© 2011 Greenhaven Press, a part of Gale, Cengage Learning

Cover image copyright © Rick Wilking/Reuters/Corbis.

LIBRARY OF CONGRESS CATALOGING-IN-PUBLICATION DATA

The U.S. economy / Jill Hamilton, book editor.
     p. cm. -- (Introducing issues with opposing viewpoints)
  Includes bibliographical references and index.
  ISBN 978-0-7377-4945-8 (hbk.)
  1. United States--Economic conditions--2009---Juvenile literature. 2. United States--Economic policy--2009---Juvenile literature. I. Hamilton, Jill. II. Title: US economy. III. Title: United States economy.
  HC106.84.U156 2010
  330.973--dc22
                                                                 2010015314

Printed in the United States of America
1 2 3 4 5 6 7 14 13 12 11 10

Contents

Foreword

Indulging in a wide spectrum of ideas, beliefs, and perspectives is a critical cornerstone of democracy. After all, it is often debates over differences of opinion, such as whether to legalize abortion, how to treat prisoners, or when to enact the death penalty, that shape our society and drive it forward. Such diversity of thought is frequently regarded as the hallmark of a healthy and civilized culture. As the Reverend Clifford Schutjer of the First Congregational Church in Mansfield, Ohio, declared in a 2001 sermon, "Surrounding oneself with only like-minded people, restricting what we listen to or read only to what we find agreeable is irresponsible. Refusing to entertain doubts once we make up our minds is a subtle but deadly form of arrogance." With this advice in mind, Introducing Issues with Opposing Viewpoints books aim to open readers' minds to the critically divergent views that comprise our world's most important debates.

Introducing Issues with Opposing Viewpoints simplifies for students the enormous and often overwhelming mass of material now available via print and electronic media. Collected in every volume is an array of opinions that captures the essence of a particular controversy or topic. Introducing Issues with Opposing Viewpoints books embody the spirit of nineteenth-century journalist Charles A. Dana's axiom: "Fight for your opinions, but do not believe that they contain the whole truth, or the only truth." Absorbing such contrasting opinions teaches students to analyze the strength of an argument and compare it to its opposition. From this process readers can inform and strengthen their own opinions, or be exposed to new information that will change their minds. Introducing Issues with Opposing Viewpoints is a mosaic of different voices. The authors are statesmen, pundits, academics, journalists, corporations, and ordinary people who have felt compelled to share their experiences and ideas in a public forum. Their words have been collected from newspapers, journals, books, speeches, interviews, and the Internet, the fastest growing body of opinionated material in the world.

Introducing Issues with Opposing Viewpoints shares many of the well-known features of its critically acclaimed parent series, Opposing Viewpoints. The articles are presented in a pro/con format, allowing readers to absorb divergent perspectives side by side. Active reading questions preface each viewpoint, requiring the student to approach the material thoughtfully and carefully. Useful charts, graphs, and cartoons supplement each article. A thorough introduction provides readers with crucial background on an issue. An annotated bibliography points the reader toward articles, books, and Web sites that contain additional information on the topic. An appendix of organizations to contact contains a wide variety of charities, nonprofit organizations, political groups, and private enterprises that each hold a position on the issue at hand. Finally, a comprehensive index allows readers to locate content quickly and efficiently.

Introducing Issues with Opposing Viewpoints is also significantly different from Opposing Viewpoints. As the series title implies, its presentation will help introduce students to the concept of opposing viewpoints and learn to use this material to aid in critical writing and debate. The series' four-color, accessible format makes the books attractive and inviting to readers of all levels. In addition, each viewpoint has been carefully edited to maximize a reader's understanding of the content. Short but thorough viewpoints capture the essence of an argument. A substantial, thought-provoking essay question placed at the end of each viewpoint asks the student to further investigate the issues raised in the viewpoint, compare and contrast two authors' arguments, or consider how one might go about forming an opinion on the topic at hand. Each viewpoint contains sidebars that include at-a-glance information and handy statistics. A Facts About section located in the back of the book further supplies students with relevant facts and figures.

Following in the tradition of the Opposing Viewpoints series, Greenhaven Press continues to provide readers with invaluable exposure to the controversial issues that shape our world. As John Stuart Mill once wrote: "The only way in which a human being can make some approach to knowing the whole of a subject is by hearing what can be said about it by persons of every variety of opinion and studying all modes in which it can be looked at by every character of mind. No wise man ever acquired his wisdom in any mode but this." It is to this principle that Introducing Issues with Opposing Viewpoints books are dedicated.

Introduction

"When America sneezes, the rest of the world catches a cold."

— Modern variation of a quote by Klemens
Von Metternich (1773–1859), "When
France has a cold, all Europe sneezes."

*I*ntroducing Issues with Opposing Viewpoints: The U.S. Economy focuses on the major issues facing America's economy. The decisions made on these issues will affect the U.S. economy today and far into the future. But the repercussions of these decisions will reach far beyond U.S. borders. The U.S. economy is an integral part of the world economy—in fact, it is the single biggest factor.

The United States is by far the largest national economy in the world. The country imports the most goods, holds the most debt, and prints the most widely used currency, the U.S. dollar. Its consumers spend the most money, and many of the world's largest and most powerful multinational corporations are based in the United States.

America's economic choices influence everything from the price per pound paid to a single coffee bean grower in Columbia to the financial well-being of entire countries. Its policies, what it buys or does not buy, and its rules on business practices help shape policies on the environment, employment practices, and product quality worldwide.

The United States is the largest importer of goods, which gives it a vast and influential buying power. If, for instance, consumers in the United States suddenly decided that they preferred organic coffee grown under fair trade conditions, this would influence factors like pricing, working standards, and environmental conditions in coffee-producing countries worldwide.

The United States also carries a huge amount of debt. Countries all over the world hold U.S. securities such as treasury bills and T-bonds. As of December 2009 Japan, America's largest creditor, held $768.8 billion in U.S. securities, according to a February 16, 2010, Department of the Treasury report. China was second, with $755.4 billion in U.S. securities. Such a tremendous debt load could lead to precarious scenarios in the future. If people lose confidence in the ability of the United States to repay its debts, the country might find itself without anyone willing to lend it money, leading to greater financial troubles. Or if the United States defaulted (did not pay its debt), the solvency of countless companies, financial institutions, and entire countries could be devastated.

Another way the United States influences world policy is through the widespread use of the U.S. dollar. The dollar is the currency most used in international transactions and constitutes more than half of other countries' official foreign exchange reserves, according to the Federal Reserve, the central bonding system of the United States. Two-thirds of the U.S. dollars in circulation are abroad, so fluctuations in the value of a dollar affect people everywhere. The prevalence of the dollar gives the Federal Reserve a vast amount of power. The organization's influence on money supply and interest rates has repercussions that echo around the world. Conversely, the power of the U.S. dollar also leaves the United States vulnerable. If confidence in the dollar falls, the U.S. economy could be devastated. "The fear is that foreigners (and Americans, too) lose confidence in its value and dump it for yen, euros, gold, or oil. If too many investors do that, a self-fulfilling stampede could trigger sell-offs in U.S. stocks and bonds," writes Robert Samuelson in an October 29, 2009, article in *Newsweek*.

But U.S. spending is the biggest factor in the world economy. The amount American consumers spend in one year is greater than the entire gross domestic product of China, India, Canada, and Russia combined. U.S. consumer spending accounts for about 70 percent of all demand in the U.S. economy, according to Ann Zimmerman and Sara Murray in the *Wall Street Journal* on August 19, 2009. Consumer spending has a massive effect on the global economy as well. U.S. consumer spending accounts for about 25 percent of the world economy, according to Knowledge@Emory from Emory University on November 13, 2008. U.S. consumer spending provides jobs, builds businesses, encourages international trade, and generally keeps the world's economy thriving.

But this tremendous amount of spending has downsides. America's massive appetite for goods is in many ways unsustainable. America's demand for cheap goods means that jobs go to countries that can provide the cheapest labor, oftentimes at the expense of worker safety and fair pay. According to Unicef, an estimated 158 million children—or one in six worldwide—are engaged in child labor, with millions working under hazardous conditions. The rush to provide cheap merchandise also can lead to poor-quality goods or goods with safety problems. In recent years several products made in China, including dog food, children's toys, and toothpaste, were recalled after they were found to be contaminated.

The massive production and consumption of goods has environmental consequences as well. The production of goods uses natural resources for manufacturing and fuel for shipping. It creates wasteful packaging and harmful by-products that pollute the air, water, and ground. And products made in countries with looser environmental rules than the United States can leave a greater environmental footprint than necessary.

The current level of U.S. spending has also taken a toll on the average American's budget. The average credit card debt per household was $8,329 at the end of 2008, according to an April 2009 Nilson Report. Sixty-one percent of Americans say they are living paycheck to paycheck, according to a 2009 study by CareerBuilder.com. And financial problems are hitting those with higher incomes, too. According to the same study, 30 percent of those earning $100,000 a year or more report living paycheck to paycheck. As Americans find their savings low, their debts high, and jobs scarce, they simply may be unable to keep up their high levels of spending.

But what if the economy rebounds and Americans are able to keep spending at high levels? Should that be a goal, or should new, more sustainable solutions be sought? Bernard Baumonl, chief global economist at the Economic Outlook Group, poses the question in the September 24, 2009, *New York Times:* "What kind of economy do we want? Should we remain perennial borrowers, where our life style continues to be dependent on the generosity of foreign lenders?" he writes, "Or has the time come for us to jettison our past shopping habits and instead focus on increasing savings and being more successful selling goods and services abroad?"

In *Introducing Issues with Opposing Viewpoints: The U.S. Economy,* the authors offer their views on the major issues facing the economy, including whether Americans should be spending more or saving more, whether green jobs are the key to a successful economic future, and whether government stimulus spending is a good or bad idea. How these issues are decided will be vitally important in shaping the U.S. economy but will also influence working conditions, the distribution of wealth and resources, and environmental conditions around the world.

Chapter 1

How Involved Should the Government Be in the Economy?

The U.S. economy involves several trillion dollars a year. Given the recent global financial crisis and the debate over health care, the question of how much the government should be involved in the economy has been brought forcefully to the public's attention.

The Stimulus Plan Is Good for the U.S. Economy

"The time for a remedy that puts Americans back to work, jump-starts our economy and invests in lasting growth is now."

Barack Obama

President Barack Obama wrote the following selection as an editorial for the *Washington Post*. When it was published in February 2009, Obama was facing a country in economic crisis and working to convince the American public that the American Recovery and Reinvestment Act of 2009 was the way out of the crisis. In this piece, Obama argues for the Recovery Act, emphasizing the improvements it would bring in health insurance, education, and infrastructure, as well as for the economy as a whole. The plan, set to cost $787 billion, met with strong opposition from Republicans—not one House Republican signed it—but it did pass. The president signed it into law on February 17, 2009, twelve days after this piece appeared.

Barack Obama, "The Action Americans Need," America.gov, February 5, 2009.

AS YOU READ, CONSIDER THE FOLLOWING QUESTIONS:
1. How many jobs does the president suggest the recovery plan will create or save?
2. Name two ways the president proposes to improve education.
3. What are three projects the president presents to "remake America for the 21st century"?

B y now, it's clear to everyone that we have inherited an economic crisis as deep and dire as any since the days of the Great Depression. Millions of jobs that Americans relied on just a year ago are gone; millions more of the nest eggs families worked so hard to build have vanished. People everywhere are worried about what tomorrow will bring.

What Americans expect from Washington is action that matches the urgency they feel in their daily lives—action that's swift, bold and wise enough for us to climb out of this crisis.

Because each day we wait to begin the work of turning our economy around, more people lose their jobs, their savings and their homes. And if nothing is done, this recession might linger for years. Our economy will lose 5 million more jobs. Unemployment will approach double digits. Our nation will sink deeper into a crisis that, at some point, we may not be able to reverse.

That's why I feel such a sense of urgency about the recovery plan before Congress. With it, we will create or save more than 3 million jobs over the next two years, provide immediate tax relief to 95 percent of American workers, ignite spending by businesses and consumers alike, and take steps to strengthen our country for years to come.

A Stategy for Long-Term Growth

This plan is more than a prescription for short-term spending—it's a strategy for America's long-term growth and opportunity in areas such as renewable energy, health care and education. And it's a strategy that will be implemented with unprecedented transparency and accountability, so Americans know where their tax dollars are going and how they are being spent.

In recent days, there have been misguided criticisms of this plan that echo the failed theories that helped lead us into this crisis—the notion that tax cuts alone will solve all our problems; that we can meet our enormous tests with half-steps and piecemeal measures; that we can ignore fundamental challenges such as energy independence and the high cost of health care and still expect our economy and our country to thrive.

I reject these theories, and so did the American people when they went to the polls in November and voted resoundingly for change. They know that we have tried it those ways for too long. And because we have, our health-care costs still rise faster than inflation. Our dependence on foreign oil still threatens our economy and our security. Our children still study in schools that put them at

At the White House, President Barack Obama meets with business leaders Anne Mulcahy (CEO of Xerox) and Eric Schmidt (CEO of Google) along with various White House advisers and staff on January 28, 2009, to discuss the economy and the benefits of the stimulus plan.

Top 10 States with the Most Jobs Created or Saved by the Recovery Act

State	Jobs created/saved	Unemployment rate
1. California	110,185.36	12.2%
2. New York	40,620.04	8.9%
3. Washington	34,517.13	9.3%
4. Florida	29,320.78	11%
5. North Carolina	28,073.32	10.9%
6. Georgia	24,681.1	10.1%
7. Illinois	24,447.55	10.6%
8. New Jersey	24,108.81	9.8%
9. Michigan	22,513.86	15.3%
10. Texas	19,571.84	8.2%

Taken from: *Recipient Reports*, Bureau of Labor Statistics. www.recovery.gov.

a disadvantage. We've seen the tragic consequences when our bridges crumble and our levees fail.

Every day, our economy gets sicker—and the time for a remedy that puts Americans back to work, jump-starts our economy and invests in lasting growth is now.

How the Plan Will Help

Now is the time to protect health insurance for the more than 8 million Americans at risk of losing their coverage and to computerize the health-care records of every American within five years, saving billions of dollars and countless lives in the process.

Now is the time to save billions by making 2 million homes and 75 percent of federal buildings more energy-efficient, and to double our capacity to generate alternative sources of energy within three years.

Now is the time to give our children every advantage they need to compete by upgrading 10,000 schools with state-of-the-art classrooms, libraries and labs; by training our teachers in math and science; and by bringing the dream of a college education within reach for millions of Americans.

And now is the time to create the jobs that remake America for the 21st century by rebuilding aging roads, bridges and levees; designing a smart electrical grid; and connecting every corner of the country to the information superhighway.

These are the actions Americans expect us to take without delay. They're patient enough to know that our economic recovery will be measured in years, not months. But they have no patience for the same old partisan gridlock that stands in the way of action while our economy continues to slide.

So we have a choice to make. We can once again let Washington's bad habits stand in the way of progress. Or we can pull together and say that in America, our destiny isn't written for us but by us. We can place good ideas ahead of old ideological battles, and a sense of purpose above the same narrow partisanship. We can act boldly to turn crisis into opportunity and, together, write the next great chapter in our history and meet the test of our time.

EVALUATING THE AUTHOR'S ARGUMENTS:

The viewpoint is written by President Barack Obama. Did you have any preexisting feelings about the president that affected how you read his words? Did his argument change your opinion, strengthen it, or leave it unchanged?

The Stimulus Plan Is Not Good for the U.S. Economy

"The administration genuinely believed, against all historical experience, that government spending would boost us out of the recession."

Rich Lowry

In the following selection Rich Lowry argues that the American Recovery and Reinvestment Act of 2009, commonly known as the stimulus plan, has been a failure. He argues that the plan was poorly timed, noting that much of the money would not be spent during 2009, in the heart of the recession. Lowry also faults the plan for putting the money into the economy in the form of tax rebates and entitlement programs. Such monies, he argues, are unlikely to do much to stimulate the economy. Lowry is the editor of the *National Review.*

AS YOU READ, CONSIDER THE FOLLOWING QUESTIONS:
1. Roughly 60 percent of the stimulus money will go to what two things, according to the author?
2. According to the author, what percentage of a temporary tax rebate will people generally spend?
3. Why is there a delay in direct government spending making it into the economy, according to the author?

Barack Obama spent all of 2008 running against the sputtering economy and warned earlier this year of a crisis "we may not be able to reverse." Yet, as the unemployment rate climbs beyond the administration's projections, Vice President Joe Biden informs us that the administration "misread how bad the economy was."

Apparently we were going to experience a once-in-a-lifetime economic crisis comparable to the Great Depression without a particularly high unemployment rate. This was the promise of the Obama administration, which indulged in hair-raisingly alarmist economic rhetoric while pumping out unduly hopeful economic projections. If the Reagan administration gave us the rosy scenario, the Obama administration has given us the rosy apocalypse.

The rosy apocalypse is an artifact of both ideological naïveté and knowing cynicism. The administration genuinely believed, against all historical experience, that government spending would boost us out of the recession. And it knew it had to assume an unrealistically rapid, robust economic recovery, because otherwise the already-horrid deficit projections would look worse. So Obama talked up the crisis to get the stimulus passed, and after that . . . happy days again!

If only the job market were cooperating. In a report prior to the passage of the stimulus, the soon-to-be head of the Council of Economic Advisers, Christina Romer, suggested the unemployment rate wouldn't increase beyond 8 percent. It now stands at 9.5 percent and will go higher. The Obama stimulus is falling victim to the poor timing and inefficiencies of all such recession-fighting spending programs.

> **Fast Fact**
>
> As of October 2009, 45 percent of stimulus award money had been given out.

Money Is Poorly Targeted

Out of the $787 billion of the stimulus, roughly 60 percent goes to individuals in temporary tax rebates and increased entitlement spending. This will provide little boost to the economy. History says that

Where the Stimulus Money Goes

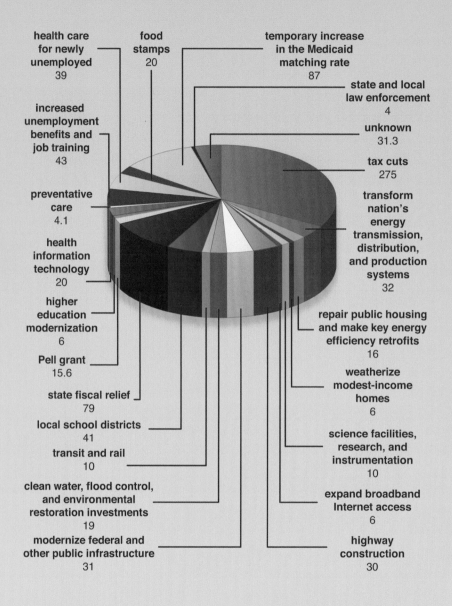

health care for newly unemployed
39

food stamps
20

temporary increase in the Medicaid matching rate
87

state and local law enforcement
4

increased unemployment benefits and job training
43

unknown
31.3

tax cuts
275

preventative care
4.1

transform nation's energy transmission, distribution, and production systems
32

health information technology
20

higher education modernization
6

repair public housing and make key energy efficiency retrofits
16

Pell grant
15.6

weatherize modest-income homes
6

state fiscal relief
79

local school districts
41

science facilities, research, and instrumentation
10

transit and rail
10

clean water, flood control, and environmental restoration investments
19

expand broadband Internet access
6

modernize federal and other public infrastructure
31

highway construction
30

*Amounts are in billions of dollars.

people will only spend 20 percent to 40 percent of a temporary tax rebate, for the very good reason that they know it's temporary.

According to the Bureau of Economic Analysis, disposable personal income increased at a healthy 1.2 percent in April and 1.6 percent in May. Is this money coursing through the economy? No, it appears most of it is being saved. In April, personal consumption declined 0.10 percent, and in May it ticked up a mere 0.20 percent. Americans refuse to spend their money as heedlessly as Obama's economic gurus hope.

The author points out that Christina Romer, chairwoman of the Council of Economic Advisers (pictured here in her Washington, D.C., office on February 4, 2009), misjudged the economy when she suggested unemployment would not reach higher than 8 percent. It has now gone higher than 9.5 percent.

Then there is the direct government spending. It will definitely make its way into the economy. The question is when. It has to run through various bureaucracies, which means delay. According to Doug Elmendorf, the head of the Congressional Budget Office, only about half of the $308 billion in spending will make it out the door by the end of fiscal year 2010 (i.e., by next September). That's about $150 billion during the next year and a half in a $14 trillion economy—in other words, a trifling 0.70 percent of the economy during that period.

Only 11 percent of that spending will take place by the end of fiscal year 2009. Most economists think the economy will be growing by the end of this year, so ideally the stimulus would begin receding in 2010 rather than taking effect in earnest. According to Elmendorf, even by the end of fiscal 2011, only 72 percent of the spending will have occurred. That means more of the spending will come in fiscal 2012 and beyond than is happening this year during the recession.

And this stimulus was touted as timely and targeted? Confronted by the inadequacies of the current program, its advocates have a predictable solution—a new one. Since the worthiest projects were presumably already covered in the first stimulus, a second stimulus would have to fund even more marginal priorities, and it would get into the economy even later. In other words, it would replicate rather than rectify the failures of the first stimulus.

Obama is resisting a second stimulus so far, but was foolish ever to go down this route. Now he's stuck hoping for the advent of his rosy apocalypse—as soon as possible.

EVALUATING THE AUTHOR'S ARGUMENTS:

The author wrote this selection five months after the Recovery Act passed. Do you think that adequate time had passed to gauge the success or failure of the plan? Why or why not?

Deficit Spending Is Necessary to Save the Economy

Mike Papantonio

"...it is going to require all those zeroes to rebuild our economy, one job, one road, one bridge, and one new technological advancement at a time."

In the following selection Mike Papantonio argues that deficit spending, while painful, is sometimes necessary to save a failing economy. He points to President Franklin Delano Roosevelt's massive spending during the Great Depression as an example of a successful use of large-scale government spending as a way to pull the country out of economic disaster. He also cites the noted economist John Maynard Keynes who, in the 1930s, championed government involvement in the economy as a way to keep the economy afloat during economic downturns. Papantonio, an attorney and author, cohosts *Ring of Fire* with Robert F. Kennedy Jr. on Air America radio.

1. What were the two points made, according to the author, by over three hundred of the world's best economists in their economic "road map" for Barack Obama?
2. The author writes that, according to economist Paul Krugman, it would take how many billions of dollars a year "to make serious inroads toward saving capitalism"?
3. The author blames twelve years of whose leadership for leading America into the Great Depression?

John Maynard Keynes was not the only world class economist who told us that huge deficit spending is imperative in order to pump life back into a recessed, depressed, catastrophically mismanaged economy.

Last month [in December 2008], more than three hundred of the world's best economists led by several Nobel Prize winners, created a road map for Barack Obama that basically said two things. First, they tell us that we have only begun to feel the pain of W's [President George W. Bush] political and economic policies. Secondly, they stated that if Obama does not undertake stellar deficit spending, America's economy will spin into a global economic catastrophe. Several of those economists, including the Nobel Prize winning economist Paul Krugman, went as far as to say that it would take as much as a steady $600 billion a year to make serious inroads toward saving capitalism. Obama is already undertaking a course of action that appears consistent with Krugman's advice. Fortunately, Obama has been a defacto president for more than a month now.

But conservative think thank geniuses, like [former Speaker of the House] Newt Gingrich—who by the way helped put us here—are telling us that the sky will fall if Obama gets his way. It shouldn't be

Fast Fact

Net interest costs paid on the public debt actually declined from $260 billion in 2008 to $199 billion in 2009 because of lower interest rates.

much of a news flash to point out to that wildly discredited crowd that W's misfit teams of political and economic advisors already have heaven crumbling down around us.

In the 1930's the political and fiscal conservatives of that time plunged America into an abysmal depression and then attacked Franklin Roosevelt when he undertook the Herculean effort to clean up their mess. Twelve years of Herbert Hoover and Warren

"When I grow up I want to be an accountant for the government, so I added the zeros to gain some experience."

Harding–style Republican presidential stewardship almost obliterated capitalism in America.

Deficit Spending Is the Way to Save Capitalism

During those years, Keynes' theory of deficit spending as a way to save capitalism was regarded as socialist witchcraft. But fortunately, FDR ignored the protests of the conservatives who brought us the Great Depression. FDR forged ahead with infrastructure and World War military spending that moved the deficit to levels that had never been seen by any nation in the world.

Similarly, Obama has inherited the deregulated, mismanaged, corrupt mess created by the Hoover-like dullards of our day, and now he already is under attack by that same crowd as he searches for a way out.

As Obama steps into this quicksand economy, he seems to realize that short-term stimulus plans are only a Band-Aid solution for a gaping, almost mortal wound. Corporate welfare money divided up among a few corrupt and inept investment bankers, and Wall Street money changers will not stop the bleeding this economy has only begun to experience.

Long-term stimulus will require astronomical levels of spending that will naturally leave us with a queasy feeling when we see all those zeroes in newsprint. But it is going to require all those zeroes to rebuild our economy, one job, one road, one bridge, and one new technological advancement at a time. According to three hundred of the world's best economists, every move Obama needs to make to save this economy will require the weight and scale of a Manhattan project [to develop the first atomic bomb] or an Apollo [space] program if we are to pull through these economic dark years still ahead.

EVALUATING THE AUTHOR'S ARGUMENTS:

The author uses a historical perspective in this viewpoint. Do you think he provides the reader with an adequate historical context for his argument?

Deficit Spending Will Leave the U.S. Economy Paralyzed by Debt

Mort Zuckerman

"Our soaring national debt will require cataclysmic adjustments to accomplish the restoration of a balance in our fiscal position."

In the following selection Mort Zuckerman argues that increasing deficit spending is a dangerous strategy for the country. He writes that more government borrowing will lead to monstrous debt payments that increase taxes and create such huge interest payments that the country will be unable to afford important programs such as defense, education, or veterans' pensions. Zuckerman is the publisher of the *New York Daily News* and editor in cheif of *U.S. News & World Report.*

AS YOU READ, CONSIDER THE FOLLOWING QUESTIONS:

1. According to the author, how much did the deficit increase from 2008 to 2009?
2. What, according to the author, will the deficit be in 2019?
3. According to a *Wall Street Journal*/NBC News poll the author cites, what is the economic issue that concerns Americans most?

The unprecedented, improbable and indeed almost unimaginable global financial crisis has virtually put an end to the comfortable notion that American and Western capitalism would dominate the world economy. In turn, the financial meltdown threatening another Great Depression has been the rationale for a phenomenal expansion of government spending to prop up demand and fend off economic disaster.

As a result, the deficit quadrupled from $459 billion in 2008 to $1.85 trillion this year [in 2009]. It has gone from 3.2% of gross domestic product [GDP] to 13.1%, twice the post–World War II record of 6% in 1983 under President Reagan. What's more, the debt surge is unlike the one that accompanied WWII in that it will not be temporary.

The nonpartisan Congressional Budget Office reckons that the deficit will run for a decade and will still exceed $1.2 trillion in 2019. By that time, the United States will have virtually doubled its national debt, to over $17 trillion. Then, after 2019, we get another turn of the screw as the peak waves of baby boomers move into their retirement years and costs soar for the major entitlements, Social Security and Medicare.

Grim Financial Projections

At 41% of GDP in 2008, the accumulated federal debt will rise to 82% by 2019. One out of every six dollars spent then by the feds will go to interest, compared with 1 in 12 dollars last year. These out-year budgets will require an increase in everyone's income taxes, raising federal income taxes an average of $11,000 for families, a hike of 55% per household—a political impossibility.

The Government Accountability Office estimates that by 2040, interest payments will absorb 30% of all revenues and entitlements will consume the rest, leaving nothing for defense, education or veterans' pensions.

If the economy would grow quickly, we might hope to pay down this debt. No such luck. The GDP trajectory is gloomy, and on top of that, the demands of special interest groups threaten to reduce growth

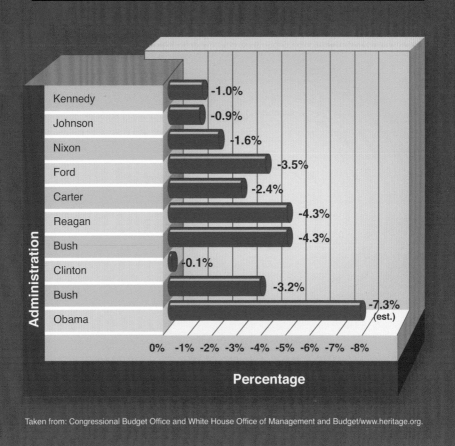

Average Federal Deficit as a Percentage of Gross Domestic Product, by Administration

Administration	Percentage
Kennedy	-1.0%
Johnson	-0.9%
Nixon	-1.6%
Ford	-3.5%
Carter	-2.4%
Reagan	-4.3%
Bush	-4.3%
Clinton	-0.1%
Bush	-3.2%
Obama	-7.3% (est.)

0% -1% -2% -3% -4% -5% -6% -7% -8%

Percentage

Taken from: Congressional Budget Office and White House Office of Management and Budget/www.heritage.org.

even more. Just look at the medical world, which pushes expensive treatments at government expense for its benefit.

American attitudes and behavior have undergone a substantial change. We are saving more and paying down debt. We are transforming our society from a consumer culture to a culture of thrift. In a recent *Wall Street Journal*/NBC News Poll, Americans were asked which economic issue facing the country concerns them the most. Deficit reduction ruled over health care. Half were prepared to defer spending or to spend less, even if it meant extending the recession.

The feeling has grown that the Obama administration is taking on too much, that the President is trying to "boil the ocean." Obama's budget is packed with a wish list of extensive new programs, especially

On January 26, 2010, in Washington, D.C., Senators Evan Bayh (D-IN) and John McCain (R-AZ) announce their bill "The Fiscal Freeze Act," which is aimed at reducing government spending and addressing the national debt.

a giant health care reform plan whose financing is thinly based. Rather than talking—optimistically—about a deficit-neutral outcome, the President should be proposing a program that reduces the cost of the most expensive health care in the world.

The public still likes Obama and recognizes his talent, but when it comes to deficit financing of programs, we have a country of "born-again budget hawks" who will rise up if taxes are boosted to pay for it all.

Deficits Mortgage America's Future

Main Street feels it will recover only when American finances are on a sounder footing. It believes that it will never recover if huge new national programs are allowed to create a monstrous structural deficit that will keep building the debt burdens far into the future to unsustainable—perhaps ruinous—heights, while a weak recovery means lower federal revenues, the piling on of more interest obligations, and thus even higher deficits.

Ruinous tax increases are inevitable if spending cuts remain outside the President's agenda.

Everybody is dazed and confused by all this talk of additional indebtedness in the trillions of dollars. Our soaring national debt will require cataclysmic adjustments to accomplish the restoration of a balance in our fiscal position.

Otherwise, we face a dramatic erosion of U.S. economic and financial standing, raising the risk of skyrocketing interest rates and a crash in the value of the dollar. Americans can no longer rely on their stocks and the soaring value of their homes to put their kids through college and support early retirement. For the first time since the Depression, U.S. companies are not only cutting jobs; they are cutting wages. We are undersaved and underpensioned, and we will have to adjust to a more frugal life.

With too much mortgage debt on their homes, too much credit card debt on their personal income, and too much overall debt, Americans have learned that they cannot continue to be borrowers.

Shakespeare had it at least half right when he said, "Neither a borrower nor a lender be." President Obama should heed [Hamlet character] Polonius.

EVALUATING THE AUTHOR'S ARGUMENTS:

Zuckerman paints a bleak financial future for America if the country takes on too much debt. Is this an effective means of persuasion, in your opinion? Why or why not?

Health Care Reform Will Help the Economy Grow

Elisabeth Jacobs

"Comprehensive health reform is critical to reviving the American economy and ensuring prosperity and growth."

In the following essay Elisabeth Jacobs argues in favor of health care reform as a way to stimulate economic growth. Fixing the health care system, she writes, will spark business innovation, ease health care costs on government, and reduce the burdens on families. Jacobs is a congressional fellow who served on the Senate Committee on Health, Education, Labor and Pensions (HELP) under Senator Edward Kennedy.

AS YOU READ, CONSIDER THE FOLLOWING QUESTIONS:

1. How much have health insurance premiums increased since 2001, according to the author?
2. According to the author, how many nonelderly Americans do not have health care?
3. What percentage of preventable illness makes up the burden of illness in the United States, according to a statistic the author cites from the Centers for Disease Control and Prevention?

President-elect Barack Obama and the 111th Congress face a historic challenge this January [2010]. The global economy is in a tailspin, our nation is at war, and the planet is in peril. In the wake of the $700-billion bailout of the struggling financial industry, many in Washington have concluded that incoming policymakers must scale back their policy aspirations, particularly with regard to health care reform. This approach is the opposite direction that President Obama and the new Congress should take.

Comprehensive health reform is critical to reviving the American economy and ensuring prosperity and growth. Without reform, rising health care costs will continue to inhibit economic growth and diminish businesses' ability to compete in a global marketplace. Workers' wages and family savings will continue to be eaten up by skyrocketing medical bills, and state and federal budgets will face increasing burdens. Reform can serve as a key that unlocks vast reserves of unrealized economic potential.

While the path to reform remains highly uncertain, the following set of arguments provide motivation for policymakers committed to forging ahead.

Health Reform Will Spark Business Innovation

- Health care costs are rising drastically for companies. In 1960, health benefits comprised just 1.2% of payroll; today they comprise 9.9%. Average employer costs for health insurance per employee hour rose from $1.60 in 1999 to $2.59 in 2005. And according to the Kaiser Family Foundation, health care premiums for employer-sponsored plans have doubled since 2000. Since 2001, health insurance premiums have increased 78%, while inflation has gone up 17%.
- The burden of health care costs on employers leaves less money for labor and capital, which means lower wages and diminished growth. For example, Starbucks spends more on health care for its workers than it does on coffee for its customers, and Kroger, a supermarket giant, has seen its health care costs rise at three to four times the rate of its revenues. Health economists estimate that a 20% increase in premiums leads to 4 million fewer jobs and a $2,000 decrease in workers' wages.
- The current health care system keeps the United States from competing effectively in the global economy. The majority of our trading

Health care workers in Los Angeles, California rally on October 20, 2009, to make 100,000 phone calls to Congress in order to urge them to pass a health care reform bill that would make health care coverage more affordable for the American public.

partners' governments sponsor guaranteed coverage for their citizens, which means that employers in these nations spend half as much on health care yet have a healthy, insured workforce. In order to compete, U.S. businesses pass those costs on to consumers, which makes American-made goods less competitive (e.g., health care costs add $1,500 to the price tag of each GM car).

- Leaving millions of Americans uninsured costs the American economy billions in lost productivity. The Institute of Medicine estimated in 2003 that the broken health care system costs the American economy $65 billion per year, or $1,645 per uninsured worker. The New American Foundation's estimates suggest that today the cost of lost productivity is $100 billion. This decreased productivity slows economic growth.

- Even workers with health insurance are less productive due to our patchwork health insurance system. Many Americans are "locked" in their current jobs because they need to maintain their existing health insurance. This means that workers' skills are not put to their best use. Some experts project that job-lock reduces workers' voluntary mobility by at least 25%. Health reform would free these workers to move into the jobs where they are most productive, which will spur economic growth.

- Effective health insurance reform will jumpstart American entrepreneurship and small businesses. Some 55% of small businesses do not offer health insurance to their workers because they simply cannot afford it, according to the National Federation of Independent Businesses. This may affect their ability to recruit the best workers, which dampens these businesses' productivity. Indeed, small businesses' health insurance costs relative to payroll increased by 30% between 2000 and 2005. By making entrepreneurship more affordable, health care reform will boost economic growth.

Health Reform Will Ease the Increasing Burden of Health Care Costs on Federal and State Budgets

- Health care costs constitute a large and growing portion of public and private expenditures. If we fail to control health care costs, federal spending on Medicare and Medicaid as a percent of GDP will double by 2030, growing from 4% to 8% of GDP. Expanding health care coverage in order to increase access to preventive care is one promising way to cut federal health care spending: $.96 of every Medicare dollar is spent on the treatment of chronic, predominantly preventable disease. Guaranteed and affordable access to preventive care could erase the majority of Medicare's costs. In the long run, healthier Americans mean a healthier fiscal balance.

Fast Fact

Corporations spent, on average, $9,552 per employee for health benefits in 2009, an increase of 6 percent from 2008.

- Escalating health insurance costs are putting an enormous burden on state budgets. Medicaid and S-CHIP [State Children's Health Insurance Program] serve as safety nets for growing numbers of working poor American families who are without health insurance. Rough economic times are further swelling the ranks of those eligible for these safety nets. As a result, states' health care costs rose by over 5% in the last year, and the Kaiser Commission on Medicaid and the Uninsured projects states' costs to increase more sharply in the coming years. Currently, burdens on state budgets are so severe that dozens of states are considering deep cuts in health care–related services. Systemic reforms that address both cost and coverage could remove a major burden from states' fiscal ledgers.

Health Reform Will Reduce Burdens on American Families and Help Spur Economic Growth?

- Workers are spending more to cover healthcare costs. In 2008, the average annual premium for a family of four was $12,680. The average employee contribution to employer-provided health insurance increased by more than 143% since 2000, and average out-of-pocket costs rose 115% during the same period. The situation is only going to worsen; a survey showed that 59% of businesses intend to increase employees' deductibles, copayments, and out-of-pocket spending limits next year.

- A broken health care system means a medical emergency quickly becomes an economic crisis for working families. When medical misfortune strikes, the typical American family faces enormous economic strain. More than 45 million non-elderly Americans (17%) do not have health insurance and must bear the full cost of a medical emergency. The current economic downturn means these numbers are likely to grow; experts project that a 1% increase in unemployment leads to 1.1 million Americans becoming uninsured. And medical bills lead to further strains on family budgets: Two-thirds (65%) of those with unpaid medical bills report problems paying for other necessities. Medical debtors report problems making mortgage and rent payments and paying for utilities; nearly half (44%) said they had used up all or most of their savings to pay their medical bills, and one-fifth (20%) said they had large credit card bills or taken out loans against their homes. Without systemic health reform, more Americans are just one illness away from economic collapse.

- Quality health care improves workers' health, boosting overall productivity and family incomes. Increased medical costs are hurting

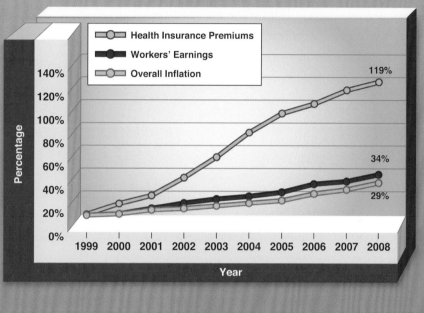

Percent Increase in Health Insurance Premiums, Inflation, and Workers' Earnings, 1999–2008

- Health Insurance Premiums
- Workers' Earnings
- Overall Inflation

119%

34%

29%

Percentage

140%
120%
100%
80%
60%
40%
20%
0%

1999 2000 2001 2002 2003 2004 2005 2006 2007 2008

Year

Taken from: The Henry J. Kaiser Family Foundation, pub. 7692-02, March 2009. www.kff.org.

health outcomes—half of Americans report that they or a family member has skipped taking prescribed medicines or postponed or cut medical care due to costs. Foregoing treatments leads to worsening health and higher incidence of illness. According to the Centers for Disease Control and Prevention, preventable illness makes up 50% of the burden of illness in the United States. Productivity losses attributable to seven common chronic (and largely preventable or manageable) diseases totaled $1 trillion in 2003. Guaranteed, affordable health insurance coverage would ensure more of these workers receive preventive care and avoid illness altogether. Millions more would be able to lead healthier, more productive lives—which means less time lost from work, reduced treatment costs for employers, and fewer lost wages for workers.

- Reform will save money for both employers and workers, which will help to stimulate the economy. Health care reforms that combine guaranteed coverage with cost-saving, quality-enhancing elements could reduce employers' health care costs by nearly $87 billion. Lower health care costs will allow employers to put more of the cost of compensation toward workers' wages and pensions. And reduced costs for workers will enable them to put more money back into other parts of the economy.

EVALUATING THE AUTHOR'S ARGUMENTS:

Instead of focusing on one particular argument and exploring all facets of it, the author presents a bulleted list supporting three main arguments to further her case. In your opinion, does this make for a stronger case? Why or why not?

Health Care Reform Will Not Help the Economy Grow

Robert A. Book

"In the long run, wasteful spending will not stimulate the overall economy or improve health care; it will only divert resources that would be better used elsewhere."

In the following essay Robert A. Book makes his case against the argument of health care reform as an economic stimulus. Proponents for health care reform as an economic stimulus, he writes, make conflicting points—that health care reform will both save money and create more jobs. Both, he argues, cannot be true at the same time. Health care reform will either save money, and in the process, eliminate jobs, or it will create jobs, and in the process, cost more. He contends that economic growth cannot come from the government moving money around in the economy but rather from creating conditions that stimulate productive activity. Book is senior research fellow in health economics in the Center for Data Analysis at the Heritage Foundation.

AS YOU READ, CONSIDER THE FOLLOWING QUESTIONS:
  1. What does the author say government spending cannot cause?
  2. Health care expenditures are forecasted to grow to almost what percentage of the GDP by 2017, according to the author?
  3. In his closing arguments, the author writes that money for increased health care spending would have to come from "somewhere." What are some of the possibilities that he lists?

A fter spending decades trying to reduce health care costs, some commentators and policymakers now argue that health care costs should be increased to stimulate the economy.

At the crux of the argument are the notions that increasing spending on health care will create jobs that can be filled by those losing jobs in other areas of the economy—and that implementing long-proposed reforms (such as an increased emphasis on primary care and large-scale deployment of health IT [information technology]) will reduce health care costs.

These two arguments are fundamentally at odds with each other. Advocates claim simultaneously that (a) it would stimulate economic growth to spend more money on these reforms, and (b) these reforms would reduce total health care costs—that is, result in spending less money. Perhaps one could make an intelligent argument for either proposition, but it is not possible to make both of those claims and be consistent.

Wasteful Spending Will Not Help the Economy

The entire proposal rests on the assumption that one can get a "free lunch" by looking at only one side of the ledger—by counting the benefits of reform but ignoring the costs. Health care jobs are clearly a benefit to workers who would otherwise have worse jobs or no jobs at all, but as long as employees need to be paid, one person's job is also another's cost. Artificially increasing the number of health care jobs also artificially (and wastefully) increases health care costs. On the other hand, reducing total health care spending means there is someone who would otherwise be paid who is either no longer being paid or being paid less—and that person is losing a job or taking a pay cut. Spending money on health care might create jobs in the health care industry but only at the cost of jobs destroyed elsewhere in the economy. In other words, health care reform might reduce health care costs, or it might create new health care jobs, but it cannot do both simultaneously.

Any money the government spends on health care (or anything else) has to come from *somewhere*—either higher taxes, more borrowing, or inflation—and that means less is available to the economy for private spending. Government spending cannot cause prosperity; it can only reallocate resources from one person or activity to another. Prosperity—economic expansion—can be achieved only by increasing total production, not simply moving it around. For this to occur, entrepreneurial individuals and companies have to find it worthwhile to engage in productive activity and investment. The only way government can induce sustainable economic expansion is to reduce the taxes and regulations that inhibit productive activity.

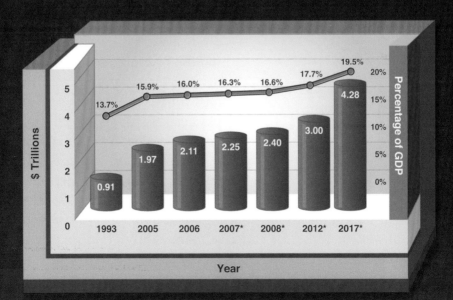

Actual and Projected National Health Expenditures for Selected Years

* = projections

Taken from: Sean Keehan, et al., "Health Spending Projections Through 2017: The Baby-Boom Generation Is Coming to Medicare," February 26, 2008. www.healthaffairs.org.

In the long run, wasteful spending will not stimulate the overall economy or improve health care; it will only divert resources that would be better used elsewhere. Health care reforms are beneficial only if they result in today's health care at lower costs, improved health care at the same or tolerably higher costs, or some combination of the two.

Increasing Spending While Cutting Spending?

Health care expenditures are taking up an ever-larger share of GDP, rising from 13.7 percent in 1993 to 16.0 percent in 2006 and forecasted to grow to almost 20 percent by 2017. Proponents of reform have long argued that this trend is sucking the lifeblood out of our economy, and bound to cause or deepen a recession. And yet, now some of those same experts are arguing that, in order to get the economy out of a recession, health care spending must be increased. In essence, it is as if they are saying, "Our economy is threatened because health care spending is too high, so to solve the problem we need to make it higher."

Fast Fact

U.S. health spending as a share of GDP in 2006 (15.3 percent) was much higher than in Canada (10 percent), France (11 percent), Germany (10.6 percent), Japan (8.1 percent), and the UK (8.4 percent).

For example, MIT economist Jonathan Gruber says that "health care reform can be an engine of job growth," and he cites two main categories of job opportunities. First, he argues that long-standing proposals for reform of primary care would create new jobs for nurse practitioners and physician assistants, which would save money because primary care is cheaper than specialty care. Second, he cites President-elect Barack Obama's proposal to spend $50 billion on health information technology, which would create jobs in the IT sector and save money through more efficient record-keeping.

However, in order for heath care reform to be "an engine of job growth," health care spending must go up, not down. After all, the main reason people like jobs is that they come with paychecks. The goal of reducing health care costs directly contradicts the "logic" of stimulus spending. The idea of stimulus through primary care reform is a contradiction: Spending will be reduced, as higher-paying specialty care jobs are replaced by lower-paying primary care jobs. Furthermore, these jobs—in serious professions requiring real expertise and years of training—would do little to improve the short-term job prospects of people laid off from other industries.

The idea that increased health IT spending will result in a permanent increase in jobs in the IT sector is a red herring [an attempt to direct attention from the real issue]. If health IT will reduce health care costs in the long run, then those new jobs in the technology sector will be more than offset by money saved—that is, jobs "lost"—in other sectors. There will be less need for file clerks and office staff and perhaps even nurses. To argue that health IT is both a good stimulus and a way to reduce health care costs is in effect arguing that it is good because it creates (technology) jobs but also good because it destroys even more (health care) jobs.

Medicaid Reform as Stimulus Spending?

Some advocate Medicaid expansion as part of a stimulus package. Medicaid is a complex program in need of reform to provide better health care for the poor at a lower cost, but there is no reason to believe that Medicaid expansion would be a source of stimulus for the overall economy. The argument that it would comes in two forms.

First, some claim that expanding Medicaid eligibility would cause previously uninsured families to spend more on consumer goods, since they would not have to save for unexpected medical expenses. Gruber and Yelowitz find that previously uninsured households that become eligible for Medicaid do indeed spend more. But this does not mean that *total* consumer spending increases—the money used to fund Medicaid expansion has to come from somewhere; in particular, whoever paid the taxes to fund the expansion had to reduce their own spending. Furthermore, the recessionary effects of taxation mean that the decrease in spending by other taxpayers is greater than the increase in spending by new Medicaid recipients.

Second, others argue that increasing federal funding for Medicaid and SCHIP [State Children's Health Insurance Program] would free up state money for public works ("roads and bridges"). In fact, it

On December 23, 2009, Republican senators Jeff Sessions from Alabama and Judd Gregg from New Hampshire discuss their view of the problems with the pending Health Care Reform legislation.

would do no such thing. These are matching fund programs: The states run the programs, and the federal government provides subsidies proportional to the funding provided by the states themselves. If the federal government gave states money to enroll more people in these programs, that would require states to spend *less* money on public works projects to meet the matching requirements. In fact, under existing law, states could already increase the amount of federal money they receive for Medicaid by choosing to spend more on their own. But they do not, because that would require cutting spending on other programs—for example, public works projects.

No Free Lunch

All of these arguments still neglect the bigger picture: Any money the federal government spends on health care reform, health IT, Medicaid, roads and bridges, or anything else has to come from *somewhere*. And that "somewhere" is either increased taxes, more borrowing, or inflation of the currency, any combination of which would cancel out any "stimulus" effect of the new spending. Spending money on health care or "roads and bridges" might create jobs in the health care or construction industries, but that is only at the cost of jobs destroyed somewhere else. This is what economists mean when they say, "There is no such thing as a free lunch."

Prosperity cannot be achieved by simply moving resources around from one sector of the economy to another. Rather, it can be achieved only by increasing production, which can be induced not by spending but by reducing the taxes and regulations that inhibit productive activity.

EVALUATING THE AUTHOR'S ARGUMENTS:

In this essay Book gives the opposing arguments and then makes his case against them. Do you think his case would be stronger if he presented only his side, or does providing the opposing view first strengthen his argument?

Chapter 2

Are Cheap Goods, Services, and Labor Good for the Economy?

Individuals and companies prefer to buy things for the lowest possible price because that reduces immediate financial costs, but are "cheap" goods and services good for the economy as a whole?

Viewpoint

1

Cheap Food Has Hidden Costs

"... if you're the one growing the food ... [y]ou're getting less for your crops, less for your work, less for your family to live on."

Timothy A. Wise

In the following viewpoint, Timothy A. Wise argues that cheap food causes hunger and has a multitude of other hidden costs. For people who buy food, such as those living in cities, cheaper food is more affordable. But for those who produce food, receiving payment for their product that is well below the cost of production means they put less food on their own tables and have less to invest in future crops. Other costs include the creation of food dependency in countries that import food and the globalization of market failure. Wise argues that cheap food comes with environmental costs as well. Wise is director of the Research and Policy Program at the Global Development and Environment Institute at Tufts University.

AS YOU READ, CONSIDER THE FOLLOWING QUESTIONS:

1. What percentage of the world depends directly or indirectly on agriculture?
2. What is market failure, and what does the globalization of market failure give us, according to the author?
3. According to the author, what are some essential things that should not be cheapened?

C heap food causes hunger.

On its face, the statement makes no sense. If food is cheaper it's more affordable and more people should be able to get an adequate diet. That is true for people who buy food, such as those living in cities. But it is quite obviously not true if you're the one growing the food. You're getting less for your crops, less for your work, less for your family to live on. That is as true for Vermont dairy farmers as it is for rice farmers in the Philippines. Dairy farmers today are getting prices for their milk that are well below their costs of production. They are putting less food on their own tables. And they are going out of business at an alarming rate. When the economic dust settles, this will leave us with fewer family farmers producing the dairy products most of us depend on.

This is the central contradiction of cheap food. Low agricultural prices cause hunger in the short term among farmers. And they cause food insecurity in the long term because they reduce both the number of farmers and the money they have to invest in producing more food.

An estimated 70% of the world's poor live in rural areas and depend either directly or indirectly on agriculture. Cheap food has made them hungry and kept them in poverty. It has also starved the countryside in the developing world of much-needed agricultural investment. Farmers have nothing to invest if they are losing money on their crops.

Wake-Up Call

The food crisis has indeed served as a wake-up call for governments and international agencies responsible for such matters. Among those most shaken from their policy slumber were officials at the World Bank, which cut the share of its spending on agricultural development from 30% in 1980 to just 6% in 2006. But, lo and behold, the World Bank's World Development Report for 2008 carried the subtitle Agriculture for Development. It was the first time in twenty-five years that the Bank had focused its signature publication on agriculture. The renewed attention was welcome, as it included a call to reinvest in smallholder agriculture, not just large-scale export crops.

The Bank, of course, studiously avoided taking any responsibility for having promoted the very policies that caused agriculture to be

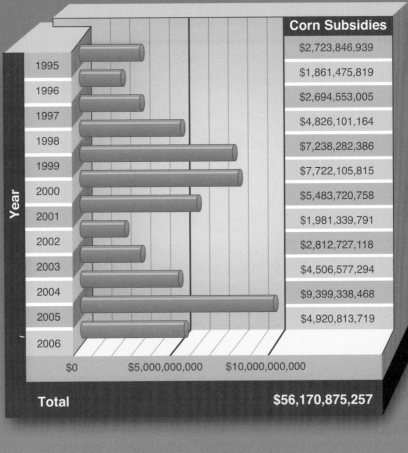

Subsidies Paid to the U.S. Corn Industry

Year	Corn Subsidies
1995	$2,723,846,939
1996	$1,861,475,819
1997	$2,694,553,005
1998	$4,826,101,164
1999	$7,238,282,386
2000	$7,722,105,815
2001	$5,483,720,758
2002	$1,981,339,791
2003	$2,812,727,118
2004	$4,506,577,294
2005	$9,399,338,468
2006	$4,920,813,719
Total	$56,170,875,257

Taken from: Farm Subsidy Database, Environmental Working Group. http://farm.ewg.org.

neglected in the first place: not only the cuts in aid and investment, but the structural adjustment programmes, imposed as conditions on its loans, which gutted the capacity of most governments to support domestic agriculture.

These same structural adjustment programmes were part of the campaign to get governments out of the economy altogether. The argument was that the market should be allowed to work its magic, to allocate resources more efficiently, to set prices without government distortions. Trade policy needed to reduce the government role as well, cutting protective tariffs and quotas and price supports, following the theory of comparative advantage.

In agriculture, what that meant for developing countries was that if you couldn't produce basic grains as efficiently—read 'cheaply'—as they could in the US, or Australia, or Brazil, you just shouldn't produce basic grains. It would be cheaper—"more efficient"—to buy them on the international market. Instead, maybe you should produce, say, flowers for export, or winter strawberries for the US market. But maybe you shouldn't produce anything because maybe your land is bad and you have no roads to get produce to a port anyway. So maybe there's nothing the market wants from you. And it doesn't need your home-grown grains any more because they are being imported.

Food Dependency

That's really how the theory works. The idea is that a country can import all the food it needs, and it should do so if it can get that food more cheaply from abroad than it could by having its own farmers grow it. One obvious problem with this approach is that if farmers stop growing food, their families don't have anything to eat, and if they can't get jobs, they have no money to buy food.

Secondly, a country can end up in a situation of food dependency, which becomes particularly problematic when prices spike and supplies get tight. That is what we saw recently with what became known as the food crisis. Countries like the Philippines couldn't get the rice they needed. They had stopped producing enough rice to protect themselves from such a market shock, and they couldn't get anyone to sell it to them because governments were concerned about feeding their own people first.

This exposed the dangers of following policies that say you can get all the cheap food you need out in the international market. A lot of countries have taken note of that; the Philippines is now on a multi-year national campaign to restore self-sufficiency in rice production.

One place where the government seems to have kept its ideological blinkers firmly in place is Mexico. There, in the birthplace of corn, where the crop was domesticated into one of the world's most important food crops, there were tortilla riots in the streets as people couldn't afford this most basic staple. In the fifteen years since the North American Free Trade Agreement took effect, US corn has flooded Mexico at prices half what it cost to produce in Mexico. Mexico now depends on imports from the US for more than a third of its corn. Some two million hungry farmers have left agriculture under the flood of cheap food.

The food crisis also illustrates what some have called the globalisation of market failure. Globalisation involves opening markets and bringing things that are produced in different parts of the world into direct competition. The assumption—and the integrity of the economic theory hinges on such assumptions—is that those markets work; that prices actually reflect the real values of what's being traded. In agriculture, the assumption is that efficiency equals high yield, which means low price, which reflects the actual value of what's produced. When it doesn't, economists call it a market failure. Agriculture is rife with market failures. You can see it in the Mexico-US trade in corn.

Fast Fact

Cheap corn is used in cheese spread, chewing gum, chocolate, instant coffee, and ketchup.

Key Areas

Environmental costs are one of the key areas where the market fails to adequately value both costs and benefits. The US specialises in environmental costs. Corn is one of the most polluting US crops of all. Excessive water and chemical use, run-off of fertilisers into waterways, the dead zone at the mouth of the Mississippi River in the Gulf of Mexico: all are examples of high environmental costs from US corn production. Producers and traders pay virtually none of the costs of those damages, and the price of corn when it goes across the border into Mexico does not reflect these environmental costs.

What happens on the Mexican side? Well, the smaller producers are maintaining great biodiversity—both wild and in corn varieties—with low-input systems. These positive contributions go unrewarded by the market. Corn biodiversity has virtually no value in the global marketplace, yet these corn seeds are the building block for future varieties of corn: ones we will need to withstand climate change, deal with pesticide resistance, and so on. The price of Mexican corn does not reflect these contributions to the common good.

When you globalise trade, you also globalise market failure. You get under-priced US corn coming into direct competition with under-valued Mexican corn. Mexican corn loses that competition, but not because it's less 'efficient'. A Mexican farmer once said, "We've been producing corn in Mexico for 8,000 years. If we don't have a comparative advantage in corn, where do we have a comparative advantage?" He's right. The problem is that comparative advantage as defined by the global marketplace doesn't value the advantage that Mexican corn offers. And in the deregulated marketplace, the only value is how cheap something is.

The globalisation of market failure gives us a worsening environment, increasing poverty among food producers, increasing food dependence, and hunger. That is why one of the main culprits of the food crisis is our blind pursuit of cheap food.

Globalisation cheapens everything. The problem is that some things just shouldn't be cheapened. The market is very good at establishing the value of many things but it is not a good substitute for human values. Societies need to determine their own human values, not let the market do it for them. There are some essential things, such as our land and the life-sustaining foods it can produce, that should not be cheapened.

EVALUATING THE AUTHOR'S ARGUMENTS:

Wise also provides the environmental costs of cheap food. Does this detract from his economic argument or enhance it in your opinion?

Cheap Food Is Necessary in Harsh Economic Times

"Dire economic circumstances don't seem to faze these spending enthusiasts, who scold us for shopping at supermarkets instead of at farmer's markets."

Charlotte Allen

In the following essay Charlotte Allen argues that cheap food is a good thing and those who disagree are "spending enthusiasts." Food writers and social critics like Michael Pollan and Alice Waters, she writes, should worry more about the effects of an increase in the price of milk on a recession-hit family rather than suggest people should be paying more for environmentally pure, locally grown food. Allen is a contributing editor to the Minding the Campus Web site for the Manhattan Institute.

AS YOU READ, CONSIDER THE FOLLOWING QUESTIONS:

1. How many jobs are lost in the United States each month, according to the author?
2. How much did the price of milk increase early in 2009, according to the author?
3. How does the author define the word *locavore*?

Charlotte Allen, "Keep Your Self-Righteous Fingers Off My Processed Food," *The Los Angeles Times,* August 30, 2009. Reproduced by permission of the author.

J ust in time for the worst economic downturn since the Depression, here comes a new crop of social critics to inform us that we're actually spending too little for the food we eat, the clothes we wear, the furniture we sit on and the gasoline that runs our automobiles.

Never mind that U.S. job losses these days range from 200,000 to 500,000 a month, that foreclosures are up 32% over this time last year and that people are re-learning how to clip newspaper coupons so as to save at the supermarket. Dire economic circumstances don't seem to faze these spending enthusiasts, who scold us for shopping at supermarkets instead of at farmer's markets, where a loaf of "artisanal" (and also "sustainable") rye bread sells for $8, ice cream for $6 a cup and organic tomatoes go for $4 a pound.

The latest cheerleader for higher prices is Ellen Ruppel Shell, a professor of science journalism at Boston University who has just published a book titled *Cheap*. It's not a guide to bargain-hunting. The theme of Shell's book, subtitled "The High Cost of Discount Culture," is "America's dangerous liaison with Cheap."

Shell's argument goes like this: Shopping at discount stores, factory outlets and, of course, Wal-Mart (no work of social criticism is complete without a drive-by shooting aimed at that chain) exploits Chinese factory workers (who would much rather be back on the collective farm wearing their Mao suits) and degrades the environment because much of the low-price junk wears out and ends up in landfills.

What Is Wrong with Low Prices?

Even IKEA comes in for a drubbing in Shell's book. Yes, the Swedish chain's inexpensive, assemble-yourself furniture may look tasteful, but behind every Billy bookcase lies a gruesome tale (in Shell's view) of Siberian forests ravaged for all that pine veneer and gallons of fossil fuel burned by couples motoring to IKEA's remote store locations, strategically chosen for their rock-bottom land values. Most damaging of all, says Shell, is the cost to America's soul.

"The economics of Cheap cramps innovation, contributes to the decline of once flourishing industries, and threatens our proud heritage of craftsmanship," she writes. In her view, we should all save up for "responsibly made quality goods," preferably from shops attainable by "public transit."

Maybe it's because I've got IKEA furniture in every room in my house (although my husband did finally lay down his Allen wrench and declare a permanent strike against "assemble-yourself," forcing us to move up the socio-furniture-nomic scale to Crate & Barrel), but I ask: What's wrong with low prices? If you don't care for the quality, well, as my mother always says, you get what you pay for.

Chefs like Alice Waters advocate the use of cooking with organic ingredients, which are expensive, but the author of this viewpoint thinks it is unrealistic for most people to use only expensive ingredients.

In an online debate with the *Atlantic*'s economies writer, Megan McArdle, Shell observes with disapproval that, when prices are adjusted for inflation, Americans today spend "40% less on clothes, 20% less on food, more than 50% less on appliances, about 95% less on owning and maintaining a car" than they did during the early 1970s.

Over that same period, Census Bureau tables show, U.S. median household income rose by at least 18% in constant dollars—despite the much-lamented (by Shell and others) decampment of "once flourishing" manufacturing jobs to China and elsewhere. That's why even America's poorest people nowadays can afford automobiles, cellphones and TVs.

Yet a significant number of social critics wish they couldn't. Robert Pollin, an economies professor at the University of Massachusetts-Amherst—cited approvingly by Shell—has argued for higher clothing prices and steep taxes on fossil fuels in the name of various social and green causes, even though, as he conceded in a January article in the *Nation*, the latter measure would "impose higher energy prices on businesses and individuals."

Food Intellectuals Are Unrealistic

The most zealous of the spend-more crowd, however, are the food intellectuals who salivated, as it were, at a steep rise in the cost of groceries earlier this year [2009], including such basics as milk and eggs. Some people might worry about the effect on recession-hit families of a 17% increase in the price of milk, but not Alice Waters, the food-activist owner of Berkeley's Chez Panisse restaurant, who shudders at the thought of sampling so much as a strawberry that hasn't been nourished by organic compost and picked that morning at a nearby farm—and thinks everyone else in America should shudder too. "Make a sacrifice on the cellphone or the third pair of Nike shoes," Waters airily informed the *New York Times* in April.

Echoing Waters was her fellow Berkeley food guru, Michael Pollan, professor of science journalism (a hot field for social critics, obviously) at UC Berkeley. Pollan (no relation to Robert Pollin) is the author of the best-selling *Omnivore's Dilemma* and coiner of the mantra "Eat food, not too much, mostly plants" that is on the lips of every foodie from Bainbridge Island to Martha's Vineyard. Pollan too rejoiced at the idea of skyrocketing prices for groceries, hoping they might "level the playing field for sustainable food that doesn't rely on fossil fuels."

Pollan also hoped that rising prices might constitute another weapon in his ongoing war against his agribusiness villain of choice: corn. Corn is a plant, of course, and thus should theoretically rank high on Pollan's list of permissible edibles. But it is also the basis of such dubious items as snack chips, Coca-Cola (high-fructose corn syrup, godfather of obesity) and suspiciously plentiful beef (corn-fed).

Pollan is a "locavore," one of those people who believe that in order to be truly ethical, you should eat only foods grown or killed within your line of sight (for me, that would be my neighbor's cat). He once described a meal he made consisting of a wild boar shot by him in the hills near his Bay Area home and laboriously turned into pate, plus bread leavened by yeast spores foraged from his backyard.

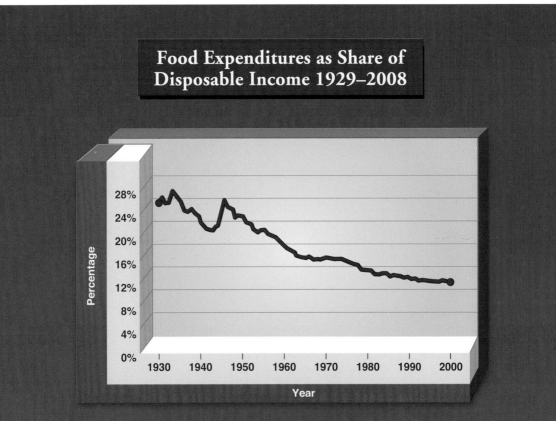

Food Expenditures as Share of Disposable Income 1929–2008

Taken from: U.S. Department of Agriculture.

Lately, Pollan has set his sights on Häagen-Dazs ice cream, not because it contains corn syrup (it doesn't) but because it's a commercially made product, and if there's one thing Pollan hates, it's commerce. His latest *pronunciamento*: "Don't buy any food you've ever seen advertised."

Demanding that other people impoverish themselves, especially these days, in the name of your pet cause—fostering craftsmanship, feeling "connected" to the land, "living more lightly on the planet" or whatever—goes way beyond Marie Antoinette saying "let them eat cake." It's more like Marie Antoinette dressing up in her shepherdess costume and holding court in a fake rustic cottage at the Petit Trianon [a chateau at the Palace of Versailles].

Those who think that there is something wrong with owning more than two pairs of sneakers or that exquisite fastidiousness about what you put into your mouth equals virtue need to be tele-transported back to, say, the Depression itself, when privation was in earnest and few people had telephones, much less cellphones. Read some 1930s memoirs: Back then, people who couldn't afford "quality" furniture slept on mattresses on the floor and hammered together makeshift tables out of orange crates. They went barefoot during the summer and sewed their children's clothes out of (non-organic) flour sacks. That was what "cheap" meant then—not today's plethora of affordable goods that the social critics would like to take away from us.

Meanwhile, Professor Pollan, eat all the "plants" you like—but don't try to pry me from my Häagen-Dazs dark chocolate ice cream. I bought it at Safeway, and it's sitting on my IKEA kitchen table.

> **EVALUATING THE AUTHOR'S ARGUMENTS:**
>
> Allen uses humor to make her argument. How, in your opinion, does this help or hurt her argument?

Viewpoint

3

Walmart Is Good for the Economy

John Semmens

"Wal-Mart is a model of how successful capitalism is supposed to work."

In the following selection, John Semmens argues that Walmart is not the "corporate criminal" it is portrayed to be. Semmens argues that Walmart provides jobs, offers lower prices so that people can buy more of what they want, fosters trade with less-developed economies, and is a good community citizen. Instead of criticizing Walmart, Semmens writes, competitors should be emulating the company. Semmens is an economist at the Laissez Faire Institute, a free-market research organization in Arizona.

AS YOU READ, CONSIDER THE FOLLOWING QUESTIONS:

1. What is the dollar amount of Walmart's annual sales, according to the article?
2. Walmart's impact on prices accounted for what percentage of the economy's productivity gains in the 1990s, according to the author?
3. In his closing arguments, the author asserts that Walmart promotes prosperity. List two of the author's arguments supporting this claim.

To some, Wal-Mart is a "corporate criminal." Loni Hancock, a California legislator, asserts that Wal-Mart's fortune "has been built on human misery." A variety of critics have accused the company of engaging in questionable and exploitive practices on its way to becoming the largest business in the world. (Its $250 billion in annual sales means that Wal-Mart has more revenues than legendary giants like Exxon, General Motors, and IBM.)

To get this big, Wal-Mart allegedly exploits its own employees by paying "poverty wages" and forcing them to work unpaid overtime. It also allegedly "squeezes" vendors, forcing them to lay off American workers and ship their jobs to foreign "sweatshops." On top of this supposed economic rapacity is the charge that Wal-Mart disregards the concerns of small communities. While such charges fuel the passions of competitors who are losing customers to Wal-Mart, unions that have been unsuccessful in organizing the company's employees, and ideologues who despise the free market, they are without merit.

Capitalism Requires Competition

The nature of competition is to produce winners and losers. Those who lose can be expected to bemoan their fate. The remedy is to improve one's own competitive offering. The strategy and tactics of the leading competitor can be observed, analyzed, and, if warranted, imitated. Countermeasures can be devised. Since competition in the free market is continuous, today's losers can be tomorrow's winners. Instead of fomenting political opposition to Wal-Mart, its rivals should be improving their own game.

Unions in America have been granted ample privileges in their quest to enlist members. Under regulations established by the National Labor Relations Board, they can convert businesses to "union shops." A union shop means the union speaks and bargains on behalf of all workers—even those who don't belong. Non-members may even be compelled to pay fees to the union for unwanted bargaining "services." The rules governing elections to determine whether a union will be instituted are slanted in favor of the union's case. If Wal-Mart employees decline to form unions they are certainly within their rights to do so.

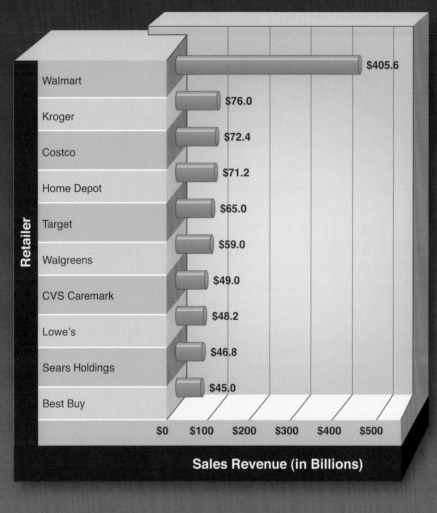

Top Retailers Ranked by 2008 Sales Revenue

Retailer	Sales Revenue (in Billions)
Walmart	$405.6
Kroger	$76.0
Costco	$72.4
Home Depot	$71.2
Target	$65.0
Walgreens	$59.0
CVS Caremark	$49.0
Lowe's	$48.2
Sears Holdings	$46.8
Best Buy	$45.0

Wal-Mart Knows It Customers

Ideologues who rant against Wal-Mart do not understand economics. In a market economy, success goes to those businesses that best and most efficiently serve consumer needs. Businesses must induce customers to hand over money in exchange for the merchandise. Customers are completely free to ignore the offerings of any business.

A customer goes through the checkout line at Walmart in San Jose, California. Walmart had a rise in profit of 17 percent in the second quarter of 2008, benefiting from low prices that attract customers experiencing financial stress in this challenging economic time.

Every business, Wal-Mart included, must win its customers' patronage anew each day.

We all know that consumers like bargains. Getting something for less money is considered savvy shopping. Wal-Mart has opted to ensure that its prices are as low as can be. This focus has enabled the company to promise "always low prices, *always.*"

Low prices benefit both the consumers and the overall economy, besides being a winning strategy for Wal-Mart. Every dollar a consumer saves on a purchase enables him or her to buy other items. More of consumers' needs and wants can be fulfilled when prices are lower than when prices are higher. Because a consumer's dollars go further at lower prices, more merchandise can be manufactured and sold. All the businesses making and selling these other products and services are helped.

The sheer size of Wal-Mart attests to the success of its strategy and the benefits to the economy. Growing into the largest business on the planet indicates that it is accurately interpreting consumer needs and efficiently serving them. This is exactly what we want businesses to do. This is what the free market encourages them to do. It is estimated that Wal-Mart's impact on prices accounted for 12 percent of the economy's productivity gains in the 1990s. This also helped reduce the effect of the Federal Reserve's inflation of the money supply.

No One Is Forced to Work for Wal-Mart

But what about the methods Wal-Mart uses to achieve its goal of low prices? What about its exploitation of labor? The free market requires that transactions be carried out voluntarily between the parties. No one is forced to work for Wal-Mart. The wages it pays must be adequate to secure the services of its employees. Would Wal-Mart's employees like to be paid more? Sure, everyone wants higher pay. If its employees could get higher pay elsewhere, Wal-Mart would lose its best workers to the businesses paying those higher wages.

The same goes for the alleged uncompensated overtime. Wal-Mart can't force its employees to work overtime without compensation. Employees are not chained to their stations. They are free to leave and take other jobs if the pay or working conditions at Wal-Mart are less than satisfactory.

Neither can Wal-Mart "squeeze" vendors, compelling them to accept deals that they would prefer to refuse. Of course, sellers would like to get as high a price for their wares as they can. Likewise, buyers would like to get as low a price as they can.

> **Fast Fact**
>
> In 2008 Walmart accounted for 43 percent of the $938 billion in revenue for the top ten retailers.

Both have to settle on a price that is mutually agreeable. Wal-Mart has a reputation for keeping its word and paying promptly. This enables its suppliers to plan their production and provides a reliable cash flow to help fund operations.

If some of Wal-Mart's suppliers choose to manufacture their products overseas, that is because doing so lowers their costs. Sure, the costs may be lower because the wages demanded by foreign workers in places like Bangladesh are low and the workplaces may be "sweatshops" compared to conditions in U.S. factories. But this is hardly the cruel exploitation that Wal-Mart's critics describe. The relevant comparison is not to the working conditions Americans have become accustomed to after two centuries of industrial progress and wealth beyond the wildest dreams of inhabitants of the less-developed countries. The relevant comparison is to the alternatives available in these less-developed economies.

Companies that employ people in factories in less-developed economies must offer a compensation package sufficient to lure them from alternative occupations. So as bad as these "sweatshop" wages and working conditions may appear to Americans who have a fabulous array of lucrative employment opportunities, they are obviously superior to the alternatives that inhabitants of less-developed economies are offered. If the "sweatshop" jobs weren't superior, people wouldn't take them.

Wal-Mart Is a Good Addition to the Community

The claim that Wal-Mart "disregards the concerns of small communities" is also contradicted by the evidence. If Wal-Mart's stores were not in tune with the concerns of shoppers in small communities, the stores wouldn't make a profit and would eventually shut down. If Wal-Mart's stores were not in tune with the concerns of job seekers in those communities, the stores wouldn't be able to staff their operations. The concerns that Wal-Mart rightly disregards are those of local businesses that would prefer not to have to deal with new competition. The absence of rigorous competition leads to high prices in many small communities. While this may be good for the profit margins of established businesses, it is not necessarily a condition to be preferred over the benefits for the majority of the inhabitants of the community that result from robust competition.

Wal-Mart runs the largest corporate cash-giving foundation in America. In 2004 Wal-Mart donated over $170 million. More than 90 percent of these donations went to charities in the communities served by Wal-Mart stores.

From an economic perspective, when all the claims are dispassionately evaluated it looks like Wal-Mart promotes prosperity. The company is helping consumers get more for their money. It is providing jobs for willing employees. It is stimulating its suppliers to achieve greater economies in manufacturing. It is encouraging trade with less-developed economies, helping the inhabitants of Third World nations to improve their standards of living. Far from "disregarding the concerns of small communities," Wal-Mart offers an appealing place to shop and work.

Wal-Mart is doing all these good things and making a profit of around $9 billion a year. This is a profit margin of less than 4 percent. That's mighty efficient. To call Wal-Mart a "corporate criminal" is slander. Wal-Mart is a model of how successful capitalism is supposed to work. It is a company that should be emulated, not reviled.

EVALUATING THE AUTHOR'S ARGUMENTS:

In his segment about the charge that Walmart underpays its workers, Semmens writes, "Employees are not chained to their stations. They are free to leave and take other jobs if the pay or working conditions at Wal-Mart are less than satisfactory." What do you think of this argument?

Discount Retailers Harm the Economy

Stacy Mitchell

"We would do well to invest more of our spending in businesses that build community wealth, rather than extract it."

Walmart and other big-box retailers are hurting workers, the economy, and local communities, argues Stacy Mitchell in the following selection. Big-box retailers, she writes, force small business owners out of business, treat their employees shoddily, sell poorly made and sometimes toxic goods, and send American manufacturing jobs overseas to countries with insufficient labor laws. This essay was written in response to a pro-Walmart column written by Katherine Kersten, a columnist for the *Minneapolis Star-Tribune.* Mitchell is a senior researcher with the Institute for Local Self-Reliance and author of *Big-Box Swindle: The True Cost of Mega-Retailers and the Fight for America's Independent Businesses.*

AS YOU READ, CONSIDER THE FOLLOWING QUESTIONS:

1. The author writes that big-box retailers have "decimated two long-standing pillars of the American middle class." To what is she referring?

Stacy Mitchell, "Low Prices, but at What Cost?" *StarTribune.com,* July 18, 2008. Reproduced by permission of the author.

2. How many jobs are lost for every new retail job created by Walmart, according to a University of California study cited by the author?
3. What is the ratio of hourly employees to store managers in a big-box store, according to the author?

Katherine Kersten tries to represent Wal-Mart as a hero of working families. But what Wal-Mart has saved poor and middle-income Americans—and there's reason to doubt the depth and durability of the discounts Kersten cites—it has taken that and more from them in diminished job opportunities and reduced income.

It's not just Wal-Mart. Rather, it's the economic model that Wal-Mart perfected and that others, including Home Depot and Target, also follow. The rise of these powerful retailers over the past 20 years has decimated two long-standing pillars of the American middle class.

One consists of small business owners, tens of thousands of whom, along with their employees, have lost their livelihoods as the big boxes have taken over.

Fast Fact

A cashier at Walmart earns an average of $7.92 an hour, below the federal poverty level.

Manufacturing workers are the other. Since 1990, the United States has lost some 3 million manufacturing jobs. Many of these losses can be traced to big-box retailers and the relentless pressure they have placed on companies to cut costs by moving to countries with low wages and lax labor laws.

Shrinking the Middle Class

Starting a small business or getting a union-wage production job provided a path out of poverty for generations of American families. No other company has done more to close these avenues to a middle-class life than Wal-Mart.

Indeed, U.S. Census data show that the middle class has lost substantial ground over the past 20 years. The share of the nation's

Walmart employees protest at the Walmart warehouse facility in Fontana, California on May 14, 2009. They are protesting low wages, the lack of health care or benefits, and the fact that the retail giant prevents them from forming a union.

income flowing to families in the middle 60 percent of the income distribution fell nearly 12 percent. The share flowing to the bottom 20 percent fell even faster, while the ranks of the working poor—people who work full time but cannot afford the basics—swelled.

Kersten points out that new Wal-Mart and Target stores often attract legions of job applicants. But this is less a sign of the desirability of these jobs than it is of widespread economic desperation. Lacking better options, more people are applying for retail work, giving the big chains a larger, and more easily exploited, labor pool.

Jobs Offer Little Hope for Advancement

Opportunities for this segment of the workforce have actually declined as the big boxes expanded. That's because the chains stretch their workers, achieving the same sales with fewer people than the businesses they replace.

David Neumark, an economist at the University of California, analyzed the impact of more than 2,000 Wal-Mart stores that opened between 1977 and 2002 and found that, for every new retail job created by Wal-Mart, 1.4 were lost as existing businesses downsized or closed.

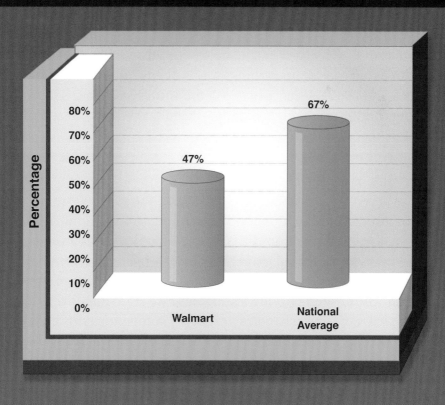

Walmart Workers Are Less Likely to Have Employer Health Insurance

Percent of workers covered by employer health insurance

Taken from: "Wal-Martization of Health Care," United Food and Commercial Workers International Union. www.ufcw.org.

Consolidation has also given these chains enough market power to hold down growth in retail wages, according to many economists.

Nor do big-box jobs offer much hope for advancement. Although a majority of store managers start as hourly workers, as Kersten notes, the ratio of store managers to hourly employees in a typical big-box store—roughly 1 to 350—makes the odds of landing on the management track incredibly slim.

Taking Advantage of Employees

Wal-Mart's vaunted logistical innovations only partly explain how it got to the top. It also got there by squeezing its employees and forcing the rest of us to pick up the tab.

Minnesota is not the only state where Wal-Mart has systematically violated labor laws by requiring employees to miss breaks and work off the clock. The retailer has lost similar suits in California, Oregon and Pennsylvania. Stealing from your own employees, especially when they make so little, is about as low as its gets.

Not surprisingly, large numbers of Wal-Mart, Home Depot and Target employees and their families, unable to make ends meet, have enrolled in Medicaid and other public assistance programs.

Do cheap DVD players make up for all this? Given the toll these companies have taken on earnings for both low- and middle-income families and the fact that prices for the things that matter most—housing, health care and education—have skyrocketed, it's hard to conclude that we are anything but worse off.

Not Such a Great Deal

There's also reason to doubt the depth and durability of those frequently touted big-box discounts. Declining product lifespans and the appalling number of products found tainted with lead and other toxins suggests that manufacturers, many of which make special lines solely for big-box retailers, may have achieved those low prices by cutting corners. We're paying less because we're getting less.

Being left with only a handful of retailers competing for our dollars is also bound to be bad for consumers in the long run. Already there's evidence that prices at Wal-Mart and other chains are higher in areas with little local competition.

Instead of shopping ourselves deeper into this economic hole, we would do well to invest more of our spending in businesses that build community wealth, rather than extract it. What characterizes such a business? Key traits to look for are local ownership, products made responsibly and even locally, and fair wages.

EVALUATING THE AUTHOR'S ARGUMENTS:

Compare this essay to the previous one. In your opinion, which one makes the stronger case for whether Walmart and other big-box retailers are good or bad for the economy?

Viewpoint

5

"How can we best tap these millions of unauthorized workers, consumers, and—yes—taxpayers as a force for economic recovery?"

Legalizing Undocumented Immigrants Would Benefit the Economy

Walter A. Ewing

In the following selection Walter A. Ewing argues that a streamlined immigrant legal-ization program is the best solution for the economy. A well-reasoned policy, he writes, would benefit the economy by keep-ing workers and taxpayers in the country, which would provide better jobs for immi-grants and bring in greater tax revenues. By contrast, the "deport them all" idea popular among strict anti-immigration groups, he argues, is not only inhumane but excessive-ly costly as well. Ewing is senior researcher at the Immigration Policy Center.

AS YOU READ, CONSIDER THE FOLLOWING QUESTIONS:

1. List two estimates from the article on the cost of deporting all unauthorized immigrants.
2. According to the article, what percentage of unauthorized immigrants pay taxes?
3. True or false: According to the author, an acceptable legaliza-tion program would require unauthorized immigrants to pass criminal background checks and pay back any past due taxes.

Walter A. Ewing, "Immigration Reform as Economic Stimulus," Immigration Policy Center, September 1, 2009. Copyright © 2009 American Immigration Council. Reproduced by permission.

The public debate over immigration reform, which all too often devolves into emotional rhetoric, could use a healthy dose of economic realism. As Congress and the White House fulfill their recent pledges to craft immigration-reform legislation in the months ahead, they must ask themselves a fundamental question: can we afford any longer to pursue a deportation-only policy that ignores economic reality? At a time when the budgets of federal, state, and local governments contain more red ink than revenue, in the midst of the worst recession since the Great Depression, what can we realistically afford to do with the roughly 12 million unauthorized-immigrant men, women, and children whom the Pew Hispanic Center estimates now live in the United States—plus the four million U.S.-born, U.S.-citizen children who have an unauthorized-immigrant parent? Even more to the point in the present economic climate, how can we best tap these millions of unauthorized workers, consumers, and—yes—taxpayers as a force for economic recovery?

There are three possible strategies for moving beyond the status quo: the fanciful "deport them all" approach still advocated by fringe anti-immigrant groups; the nebulous [vague] "attrition through enforcement" approach now advocated by mainstream anti-immigrant groups; and the creation of a program under which unauthorized immigrants could apply for legal status—an approach advocated by a wide array of groups on pragmatic, economic, and humanitarian grounds. In contrast to the first two options, the legalization approach represents an acknowledgment that enforcement measures alone cannot fix a problem that was caused in large part by a decades-long mismatch between legal limits on immigration and the actual labor demands of the U.S. economy. Just as importantly, though, legalization also acknowledges the fact that, since the U.S. economy is now in recession, incorporating currently unauthorized immigrants into our strategy for economic recovery makes far more fiscal sense than spending untold billions of

> **Fast Fact**
>
> The number of unauthorized immigrants in the United States is estimated to be between 12 and 20 million.

dollars, in the middle of multiple budget crises, in a quixotic [idealistic or unrealistic] quest to force them all out of the country.

"Deport Them All"?

The "deport them all" scenario is, obviously, the most unrealistic. Leaving aside the daunting logistical, legal, and civil-rights issues involved in raiding homes, schools, and worksites around the country in search of unauthorized immigrants, what would a mass-deportation campaign cost? Julie L. Myers, head of Immigration and Customs Enforcement (ICE) during the Bush administration, told Senators during her confirmation hearing in 2007 that it would cost at least $94 billion; a figure which ICE subsequently noted did not include the cost of actually finding unauthorized immigrants, nor the court costs associated with deporting them. The Center for American Progress (CAP) released a more comprehensive estimate in 2005 that put the price of mass deportations at somewhere in the range of $206 billion to $230 billion over five years.

Wearing a President Obama mask, Anthony Marquez participates in a rally for immigration reform in Los Angeles, California on May 1, 2009. The rally is pushing for immigration laws to legalize the more than 12 million immigrants who are in the United States illegally.

Suffice it to say that deporting 12 million-plus people would not be cheap. And neither the ICE nor the CAP estimates even begin to account for the economic impact on numerous businesses of suddenly losing the workers who make their products or the consumers who buy them. A 2008 report from The Perryman Group estimated that, were all unauthorized workers and consumers somehow removed from the country, the United States would *lose* $551.6 billion in annual spending, $245 billion in annual economic output, and more than 2.8 million jobs. Moreover, federal and state treasuries would lose the revenue they now receive from unauthorized taxpayers. (Contrary to popular opinion, between half and three-quarters of unauthorized immigrants pay federal and state taxes, according to the 2005 *Economic Report of the President.*)

As opposed to the brute force of mass deportations, the goal of "attrition through enforcement" is to make life in the United States so difficult for unauthorized immigrants that they choose to leave, or "self-deport." This approach involves several types of immigration enforcement (including the construction of an expensive and ineffective U.S.-Mexico border fence, which Congress still seems intent upon pursuing). But the centerpiece of the effort would be the mandatory, nationwide implementation of the federal government's now-voluntary "E-Verify" system, through which employers check new hires against the databases of the Social Security Administration (SSA) and Department of Homeland Security in an attempt to ensure that they are authorized to work in the United States.

Self-Deportation Is Also Unrealistic

In addition to the question of how much it might cost to make E-Verify mandatory for all employers, there is also the question of whether or not it stands a good chance of actually working. In other words, how likely is it that E-Verify would make it so difficult for unauthorized immigrants to find a job that they would leave the country? Reports by the federal government's own researchers do not bode well with regard to either the effectiveness or cost of a nationwide E-Verify program.

The Government Accountability Office (GAO) reported to Congress in 2005 that E-Verify cannot detect identity fraud in which an unauthorized worker presents an employer with either valid identity documents belonging to another person, or reasonably well-made counterfeit documents containing valid information about another person. The SSA Inspector General reported to Congress in 2006 that the Social Security records of about 12.7 million native-born U.S. citizens probably contain errors that would "result in incorrect feedback" to employers as to their identity or authorization to work. And CBO estimated that the mandatory E-Verify system called for in the SAVE Act of 2007 would have cost at least $12 billion over 10 years to implement, and probably would have also *decreased* federal revenue by $17.3 billion over the same period as *more* workers were paid under the table, outside of the tax system.

In other words, implementing E-Verify nationwide would cost tens of billions of dollars, would not detect identity fraud, would incorrectly flag millions of U.S. citizens as not being who they say they are, and would result in less tax revenue being collected from unauthorized workers than is now the case. None of these outcomes seems particularly desirable at a time of high unemployment and gaping budget deficits. Nor does this seem to be a promising means of persuading unauthorized immigrants to self-deport.

Legalization Is Best

The third option—creation of a legalization program—would require unauthorized immigrants to pass criminal background checks and pay fines, fees, and any back taxes they might owe. The relative cost-effectiveness of this option is apparent in a CBO analysis of the Comprehensive Immigration Reform Act of 2006—which preceded the onset of the current recession and therefore included increases in legal limits on future immigration as well as a legalization program for unauthorized immigrants already in the country. CBO estimated that the bill would have generated $66 billion in new revenue over 10 years, primarily from income and payroll taxes paid by both new and newly legalized immigrants. This revenue would have more than offset the anticipated $54 billion increase in spending for refundable tax credits, Medicaid, Medicare, Social Security, and food stamps for newly eligible immigrants and their families during the same period.

Given the current condition of the U.S. economy and the federal treasury, what makes more sense? Spending tens of billions of dollars trying to force, or forcefully persuade, millions of unauthorized dishwashers, nannies, and gardeners to uproot millions of U.S.-citizen children and leave the country? Or create a legalization program which weeds out the very few unauthorized immigrants who might be dangerous criminals, and then ensures that the rest are paying into the tax system? Does it make more sense to take unauthorized consumers and taxpayers out of the economy, or—by allowing them to earn legal status—enable them to earn higher wages and therefore spend more and pay more in taxes?

EVALUATING THE AUTHOR'S ARGUMENTS:

Ewing argues his case for legalization of unauthorized immigrants on economic grounds. The legalization debate also has humanitarian and social elements. Would Ewing's case have been strengthened or weakened by including these other elements, in your opinion?

Legalizing Undocumented Immigrants Would Not Be an Economic Stimulus

"An amnesty would be costly and would encourage more individuals to cross over the border illegally."

Jena Baker McNeill

In the following selection Jena Baker McNeill argues that providing sweeping amnesty for illegal immigrants would not be an economic stimulus and that Congress should take a more incremental approach. She advocates a variety of strategies, including keeping the border secure, enhancing legal worker programs, and promoting economic development and good government in Latin America. McNeill is policy analyst for homeland security at the Heritage Foundation.

AS YOU READ, CONSIDER THE FOLLOWING QUESTIONS:

1. The author lists three reasons she believes legalizing immigration is not the answer. What are they?
2. How does the author define low-skill immigrant households?
3. What are the five alternative approaches to legalization that the author recommends?

On April 30 [2009], the U.S. Senate Judiciary Committee, Subcommittee on Immigration, Border Security, and Citizenship, held a hearing to examine the question: "Comprehensive Immigration Reform in 2009: Can We Do It and How?"

While the consensus of the panel was that comprehensive immigration reform should be part of Congress's legislative agenda in the near future, one only need to look at previous failed attempts at a comprehensive solution to determine that this approach will not work. All too often, comprehensive reform has become a metaphor for amnesty and has done little except encourage more individuals to come to the U.S. illegally.

Effective change does not require Congress to pass a massive, comprehensive immigration bill. Rather, Congress needs to fix immigration in a more incremental manner that is designed to:

- Reduce the incentives for illegal immigration; and
- Strengthen employers' ability to hire the employees they need to help the economy grow without jeopardizing the nation's security, sovereignty, and social fabric.

Fast Fact

The top five states estimated to have the most unauthorized immigrants are California, Texas, Florida, Illinois, and New York.

This approach would include:

- Safeguarding the southern border,
- Promoting economic development and good governance in Latin America,
- Enhancing legal worker programs,
- Reforming U.S. Citizenship and Immigration Services (USCIS), and
- Enforcing immigration and workplace laws.

Legalization Is Not the Answer

The idea that legalization is the best solution to America's immigration problem is being suggested with increasing frequency. In fact, the Senate hearing's witnesses, including Alan Greenspan, seemed

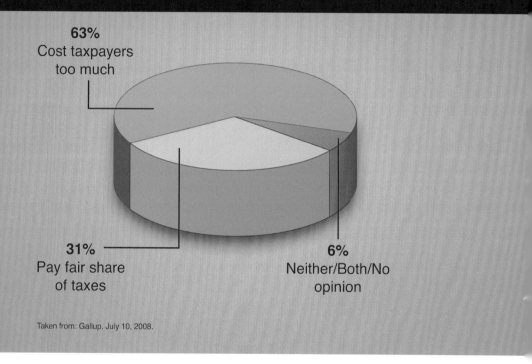

Americans Are Divided on Whether Illegal Immigrants Become Productive Citizens or Cost Taxpayers Too Much by Using Government Services

Which comes closer to your point of view: Illegal immigrants in the long run become productive citizens and pay their fair share of taxes, or illegal immigrants cost the taxpayers too much by using government services like public education and medical services?

63%
Cost taxpayers too much

31%
Pay fair share of taxes

6%
Neither/Both/No opinion

Taken from: Gallup, July 10, 2008.

to suggest the idea that legalization would somehow be an economic stimulus. But this policy of amnesty first and security and enforcement later is a recipe for disaster that would only hurt the nation. Legalization is not the answer for the following reasons:

- *It Is Not an Economic Stimulus.* Despite the claims that legalization would be an economic stimulus, the reality is that such a decision would be very costly to the United States. While it is true that immigrants generally add to the economy, there has been a flood of low-skill, low-educated migrants, most of whom have come to the country illegally and many of whom bring with them similarly educated and skilled family members. These migrants use public services, health care facilities, and schools while paying few of the taxes that support these public sector activities—at a very high price tag.

Overall, households headed by immigrants without a high school diploma (or low-skill immigrant households) received an average of $30,160 per household in direct benefits, means-tested benefits, education, and population-based services in FY 2004. This cost would far exceed the economic benefits of legalization.

- *It Erodes Rule of Law.* Rewarding those who came into the U.S. illegally would encourage others to engage in same behavior.
- *It Threatens Immigrant Safety.* Amnesty would encourage more people to cross the border illegally in hopes of staying in the United States without repercussion. Crossing the southern border, however, is highly dangerous—there are many hazards, including border smugglers who often rape and murder those they pretend to help. The U.S. should not provide an incentive for more people to take this dangerous journey.

An Alternative Approach

Legalization of the individuals illegally in the United States is not the right approach to solving America's immigration problem. Those who support legalization have attempted to characterize dealing with illegal immigration as a choice between permanent legalization and the forced deportation of each and every illegal immigrant in the United States, but there are other options.

Congress needs to move beyond the idea of a comprehensive approach to immigration reform and instead adopt a segmented strategy that addresses each element of the problem individually. A new strategy should do the following:

- *Keep the Border Secure.* The Bush Administration started the process of deploying new agents and more technologies while erecting physical barriers. This was an important first step. Now the Obama Administration should continue these measures in a way that is in line with the operational needs of the Department

U.S. Border Patrol Agent Roy Salinas searches an illegal immigrant in Nogales, Arizona on April 6, 2006. Some proposals for immigration reform would add thousands of agents to patrol the border.

of Homeland Security. Also, these efforts need to be integrated with state and local governments, as well as private citizens, by supporting Border Enforcement Security Taskforces and State Defense Forces.

- *Promote Economic Development and Good Governance in Latin America.* Tackling the illegal immigration problem starts with reducing the pressure on citizens to come to the U.S. illegally. This pressure is primarily the result of a lack of employment opportunities in Latin America. Aiding Latin American countries in their economic development will greatly reduce the pressure on their citizens to come to the U.S. illegally. Furthermore, in Mexico it is vital that the U.S. help the Mexican government combat the drug cartels that are trying to destabilize that nation.
- *Enhance Legal Worker Programs.* The United States has always been a destination for immigrants and requires a robust and efficient visa system. Faulty visa programs have encouraged many employers and immigrants to resort to illegal immigration.

The U.S. needs to provide legal avenues that meet the needs of employers and immigrants and provide a better alternative than illegal immigration.

- *Reform USCIS.* As of now, USCIS could not handle a surge of legal immigrants, in part because it has a faulty budget model based on application fees. For USCIS to be responsive to immigration reform, its revenue structure should be changed to give the USCIS more flexibility. This can be accomplished by investing in workplace enforcement and by establishing a national trust fund to pay for programs for which USCIS cannot charge fees—for example, amnesty applications and naturalization of military personnel.

- *Enforce Immigration and Workplace Laws.* Homeland Security Secretary [Janet] Napolitano must ensure that internal enforcement efforts continue. This includes workplace raids that help to decrease incentives for both illegal immigrants and employers, as well as 287(g) programs, which help state and local law enforcement enforce immigration laws.

Time for a Different Approach

Repackaging amnesty as an economic stimulus does not dilute its terrible effects. And legalizing immigrants here illegally would not provide an economic boost. In fact, an amnesty would be costly and would encourage more individuals to cross over the border illegally—which is a threat to their safety—without solving the problem.

It is time for Congress to take a different approach to immigration reform, one that upholds the rule of law, respects the needs of the economy, and provides a legal means by which to come to the U.S.

EVALUATING THE AUTHOR'S ARGUMENTS:

McNeill presents her arguments in a list, with a bullet by each point. Does this presentation affect how you read the argument? How?

Chapter 3

What Can Help the U.S. Economy?

U.S. Treasury Secretary Timothy Geithner with Peter Orszag (Office of Management and Budget Director) and Christina Romer (Chairwoman of the Council of Economic Advisers) testify on the 2011 fiscal year Budget and Economic Outlook in Washington, D.C. on March 16, 2010.

Viewpoint

1

Americans Need to Save More to Strengthen the Nation's Economy

Alejandra Lopez-Fernandini

"Having accessible savings is critical to our personal and economic security."

Americans need to save more than ever during a recession, argues Alejandra Lopez-Fernandini in the following selection. Saving offers people a cushion for hard times and helps pay for future needs like a home, education, and retirement, she writes. Saving is so crucial, she argues, it should be aggressively encouraged through programs like Children's Saving Accounts and automatic enrollment in employee savings accounts. Lopez-Fernandini is a senior policy analyst in the Asset Building Program at the New America Foundation, a Washington-based think tank that "seeks innovative solutions across the political spectrum."

AS YOU READ, CONSIDER THE FOLLOWING QUESTIONS:
1. How did the United States rank in its rate of personal savings with the other nineteen major industrialized economies, according to the author?
2. Name one reason the author gives that it is important that "we save more as a nation."
3. What is a Children's Savings Account, as described in the article?

As the economy slows, millions of Americans will cut their budgets to stay afloat. This generates conflicting impulses: If I skip that morning coffee and granola, will my thriftiness put my local coffee shop out of business?

Will that force America's granola farmers to lay off workers? What's a budget-conscious, patriotic and hungry girl to do?

Not to worry, saving a few dollars now will not prolong the recession. And, more important, spending all your discretionary income will not end the recession.

It's true that [economist] John Maynard Keynes' "Paradox of Thrift" suggests that, even while saving is beneficial to an individual, too much aggregate savings could deepen an ordinary recession. But in these extraordinary times, where banks and not just businesses are in desperate need of cash, this economic rule may not fully hold.

Now Is the Time to Save

More important, individuals need savings to be prepared for unanticipated expenses and income losses, especially now. The reality is that there is no bailout coming to you. And those getting the bailout might not be willing to lend to you, anyway. So now is the time to save.

The money you save is your own personal safety net, what you tap when you have an unanticipated expense like a car repair or when you're between jobs, as many Americans find themselves nowadays.

The past decade has seen Americans saving at historically low levels; we've substituted plastic for the piggy bank. But the days of cheap and easy access to credit have come and gone. We all need to save not because we want to but because we have to.

America Is in "a Precarious Position"

For decades, our country's economy has flourished, but it relied too heavily on debt-driven consumer spending to power its growth. Excessive household debt, coupled with stagnating incomes and little to no personal savings, now places America in a precarious position.

The author of this viewpoint urges Americans to save more money, as this young woman is doing by putting money into a piggy bank, historically a symbol of thrift.

Compared with the 19 other major industrialized economies, the United States ranks dead last for personal savings. That's right, in 2003, the United States was the least thrifty nation among the G-20.

Why is it important that we save more as a nation? Savings offers us the protection we need to make it through hard or uncertain times and to pay for important future needs such as a home, education or adequate retirement. Savings also creates pools of capital for investment purposes (who will fund the next neighborhood coffee shop?) and to keep interest rates low.

It appears the current recession has scared us back to saving; we are no longer spending all of our disposable income. To ensure that the hopeful trend continues, government and employers should adopt a new generation of savings policies that are both innovative and simple.

Why We Do Not Save

Common sense, along with research from the emerging field of behavioral economics, tells us why we aren't saving more already:

1) *We like instant gratification.* Whether it's iPhones or our paychecks, we want everything, and we want it now. We are so short-term-oriented that many of us would rather have a fatter paycheck now than set aside some of that happiness, even if the funds will be greater in the future.

2) *We tend to procrastinate.* Once we start something (or fail to start something), it's really hard to change course. And we'd prefer a hassle-free world. Who doesn't, right? When it's hard just to figure out how to start saving, most people won't. However, the flip side is that when it's easy to start saving, a lot more people will. Think about current retirement savings. How many of us would open an account and make regular deposits if an employer didn't take it right out of our paychecks?

Making It Easier to Save

When it comes to savings, we need someone to save us from ourselves. Smart savings policies should be automatic and utilize smart pre-made choices, or defaults. It would require action to *not* save. Of course, this type of policymaking underscores the importance of making the default choice a good one (an adjustable-rate mortgage with no down payment would be an example of a bad default).

Employers can easily help their employees save for a rainy day, leveraging the payroll system and direct deposit to automatically send a small percentage of their paychecks to a savings account. This type of unrestricted savings is especially valuable for individuals who have limited liquid assets and who may otherwise be forced to meet emergency cash needs with high-cost payday loans.

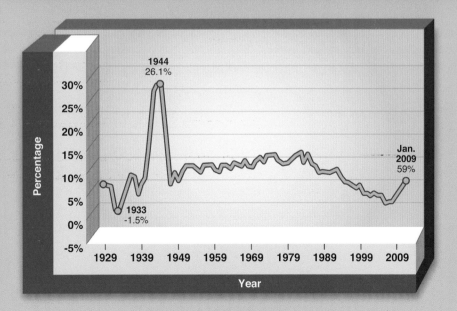

Savings on the Rise

Personal savings rate as a share of disposable personal income, 1929–2009

A truly transformative savings policy to broaden the base of American savers would encourage it from birth with Children's Savings Accounts. These "start in life" accounts would be "seeded" up-front with a modest initial deposit ($500), progressively funded for children born into lower-income households and restricted for specific asset-building uses like higher education, purchasing a home or starting a small business.

For the economic health of the next generation, the United States should join the U.K. and Singapore, and others who are offering such lifelong savings accounts, and get some skin in the thrift game, too.

We know it's plenty hard to save; it feels a lot like we're taking away what we've rightly earned. Taking advantage of windfall payments such as tax refunds is important, and so is removing the temptation to spend all of that refund. Tax filers can pre-commit a portion of their refund before it reaches their pocket to up to three accounts (including savings accounts!) with IRS Form 8888.

Having accessible savings is critical to our personal and economic security. We must reorient the savings policy discussion to include the needs of shorter-term savers and consider policy that would make savings automatic and universal at birth.

> **EVALUATING THE AUTHOR'S ARGUMENTS:**
>
> The author uses a casual, conversational tone in making her argument. In your opinion, does this diminish her argument or make it more accessible?

Americans Are Saving Too Much and Making the Recession Worse

David Fessler

"This situation could feed on itself and things could get even worse."

In the following essay David Fessler argues that when Americans save too much, they fuel the recession. He cites the famous British economist John Maynard Keynes, who developed the concept of the "paradox of thrift." The idea is that when consumers stop spending and start saving, the demand for goods and services is reduced, thus slowing the economy. Money needs to be reintroduced into the economy to keep it growing, he writes, but the United States is running out of places to get that money. Fessler is an advisory panelist for the Oxford Club, a network of private investors.

AS YOU READ, CONSIDER THE FOLLOWING QUESTIONS:

1. The savings rate jumped how much from 2008 to 2009, according to a Bureau of Economic Analysis study cited by the author?
2. What dollar value does the author assign to the U.S. economy?
3. Who does the author say is financing the government's stimulus spending plan?

W e've all heard this from our parents: *"Spend what's left after saving, instead of saving what's left after spending."*

Or perhaps this was drummed into your head: *"Always save for a rainy day."*

The idea of saving didn't just start with our parents' generation, however. Ben Franklin was giving advice on saving way back in 1732 in *Poor Richard's Almanac*: *"If you would be wealthy, think of saving as well as getting. Creditors have better memories than debtors."*

As the recession of 2008 hit, Americans suddenly stopped spending, paid down their debts and started saving—some for the first time in their *lives*. . . . As a result, America's savings rate—as a percent of disposable income—has leapt from a little over 1% to over 5% in just the last 18 months [from 2008 to 2009] according to the Bureau of Economic Analysis (BEA).

At first glance, things would seem to be improving. But there's a sinister force at work here. It's called the "paradox of thrift"—and it's sending America to the poorhouse.

Fast Fact

The personal savings rate increased while corporate and government savings rates decreased from 2007 to 2009.

The Paradox of Thrift

So what is the "paradox of thrift" exactly?

It's a concept that was popularized by John Maynard Keynes, a famous British economist whose ideas have had a major influence on modern economics. It goes something like this: *When consumers stop spending and start saving, the overall demand for products and services drops and unemployment rises. In turn, this causes the overall nationwide savings rate to drop because of the decrease in consumption and the slower economic growth that ensues.*

One can therefore draw the conclusion that an increase in savings is harmful to the overall economy. Think of it this way: If a person stops spending, he or she is affecting someone else's income, and their ability to spend, and so on.

You could also conclude that this situation could feed on itself and things could get even worse: More savings . . . even less consumption . . . more unemployment, etc. And if nothing drastic is done, it will.

So what are the options?

Can Other Countries Help?

For a start, how about other countries picking up where we left off?

With different countries in different stages of development, it stands to reason that some are in the consumption stage and could pick up the slack where the United States left off back in 2007.

There's just one problem: The U.S. economy is a $14 trillion-per-year juggernaut [an overwhelming force], and all the developing countries in the world put together don't come anywhere close.

Bottom line: The ability of developing nations to step up their spending wouldn't adequately balance out the increased savings going on here in the United States.

So if international consumers can't (or won't) spend money fast enough to reverse the trend, then who will? If you guessed Uncle Sam . . . bingo! Thing is, governments in other countries are in the same boat we are. . . .

The "paradox of thrift" demands that money be spent in order to reverse the current downward trend brought on by the drop-off in consumer spending and the drastic increase in individual savings.

"The Paradox of Thrift," illustration by Tom Fishburne, TomFishburne.com, 2009. Copyright © 2009 Tom Fishburne.

Will it work? According to CNBC economist Steve Leesman, any time the government introduces money into the system and increases the deficit, resident and non-resident spending increases to keep pace. This will increase the demand for products and services, so manufacturers will have to hire people in order to meet the increased demand, and that will beget even more spending, more hiring, etc.

However, this approach is highly controversial and political. And in some people's minds, it's just laying the groundwork for the next financial meltdown.

Is Spending the Only Solution?

So are we destined to keep repeating this spending cycle in order to grow as a nation?

The answer is "no." But here's the real problem: Foreign investors are financing the U.S. government's massive economic stimulus spending plan. And while foreigners are content to continue buying U.S. dollars for now, they're tiring of Uncle Sam and his lavish spending habits—and they're beginning to look elsewhere for places to park their cash.

The bottom line is this: The current process of deficit spending is unsustainable. The U.S. government—like the rest of us—has to begin to pay down its debt.

Sure, it's a painful process for governments, just as it is for individuals. But in the long run, the paradox of thrift won't be a paradox at all. Higher savings will indeed lead to greater investment and prosperity.

As another old saying goes, "Frugality is its own reward."

EVALUATING THE AUTHOR'S ARGUMENTS:

Compare this essay to the previous one that urged Americans to save more. Which do you think made the better argument? Why?

Green Jobs Are the Future of the Economy

Christopher Weber

"Green-collar jobs are already a growing part of the U.S. economy."

In the following viewpoint, Christopher Weber discusses the potential of green-collar jobs to aid in the recovery of the U.S. economy. Weber points out that green jobs are not just for the future—they are a current and growing part of the U.S. economy. Plans discussed suggest that green jobs would not only benefit the environment, but they could create millions of jobs and free up funds from energy production for more important tasks such as education and patient care. The growth of a green economy could also be an opportunity to address social and economic injustices, but this is not guaranteed. Weber is a journalist and contributor to *In These Times*, a politically progressive magazine.

AS YOU READ, CONSIDER THE FOLLOWING QUESTIONS:

1. What is a green-collar worker?
2. In what areas would half of the jobs that are created be in, according to the article?
3. According to Weber, what has Obama promised to include in federal job-training programs?

Until recently, most people had never heard of "green-collar jobs." Yet the phrase is suddenly on policymakers' tongues... Green-collar jobs are already a growing part of the U.S. economy. As demand has risen for clean energy and environmentally responsible manufacturing, workers are turning out everything from hybrid cars to organic cotton underwear.

In most scenarios, a green-collar worker is one who translates new environmental technologies for consumers, designing and manufacturing goods that use fewer materials and less energy than those of just a few years ago. Environmental groups from the Sierra Club to the League of Conservation Voters say these jobs are a victory for the environment and for workers.

"This is a great time for us to ramp up the level of investment in clean energy," says Pete Altman, climate campaign director for the Natural Resources Defense Council (NRDC). "Significantly more people can be employed in energy-efficiency retrofits and building wind and solar plants per dollar invested than just buying natural gas or oil or coal."

One of the grandest election promises—aside from liberating the nation from foreign oil—was to create a sizeable pool of new jobs. On the campaign trail, Obama offered a plan to create 5 million green-collar jobs over 10 years. He promised to support this initiative with $150 billion from the federal coffers.

During his Dec. 6 address, Obama condensed the proposed timeframe for this green investment to two years. He outlined green jobs and infrastructure improvements as part of his much larger economic stimulus plan intended to jolt the anemic U.S. economy. Up to $100 billion would go to upgrading the nation's infrastructure, with schools, hospitals and communication systems targeted for "green" improvements.

At the same time, more radical visions for the green economy are gaining support. Two progressive think tanks, the Center for American Progress (CAP) and the Apollo Alliance, have argued for "green recovery" plans—economic roadmaps that emphasize the key role of green jobs.

Key Role of Green Jobs

CAP commissioned a study by the Political Economy Research Institute at the University of Massachusetts-Amherst. Unveiled in

September, "Green Recovery: A Plan to Create Good Jobs and Start Building a Low-Carbon Economy" urges investment in retrofitting buildings for energy efficiency; expanding public transit and freight rail; building a cutting-edge electrical grid; and developing wind, solar and biofuel energy. It also notes:

> Public and private investment in energy efficiency reduces energy demand and lowers energy costs. . . . Lowering energy costs for educational buildings eventually means more funds for teachers, books and scholarships. Retrofitting hospitals over time releases money for better patient care.

These improvements will lead to the creation of 2 million jobs in two years, according to the study's authors, Robert Pollin, Heidi Garrett-Peltier, James Heintz and Helen Scharber. About half of the jobs would be in construction and manufacturing. The rest would

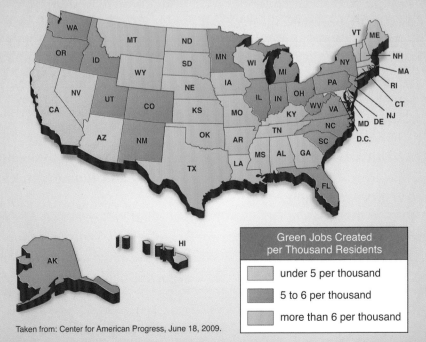

Energy and Job Creation

According to the Center for American Progress, an investment of $150 billion for clean energy would create 1.7 million jobs.

Green Jobs Created per Thousand Residents

- under 5 per thousand
- 5 to 6 per thousand
- more than 6 per thousand

Taken from: Center for American Progress, June 18, 2009.

come as suppliers, retail and other industries ramp up behind this growth. All told, the authors estimate that their approach would cost taxpayers about $100 billon over two years.

Several unions, including the AFL-CIO, support an aggressive stimulus like the one proposed by the study.

Fast Fact

The average green job in North America pays $99,995, according to the Carbon Salary Survey.

"I think everybody in the labor movement recognizes that we have to make this economy more sustainable as well as more just," says Ron Blackwell, AFL-CIO chief economist. "The particular challenge is to make the transition to a greener economy in a way that does not impose disproportionate costs on working families. . . ."

Green Economy Needs to Address Injustices

Van Jones, founder and president of the advocacy group Green for All, argues that the new economy must address social and economic injustices. In his book, *The Green-Collar Economy*, Jones writes that green jobs can uplift marginalized workers:

> The green economy should not just be about reclaiming thrown-away stuff. It should be about reclaiming thrown-away communities. . . . Formerly incarcerated people deserve a second shot at life—and all obstacles to their being able to find that second chance in the green sector should be removed. Also, our urban youth deserve the opportunity to be part of something promising. Across this nation, let's honor the cry of youth in Oakland, Calif., for "green jobs, not jails."

Activists and local politicians are now building training programs so that low-income workers, people of color and immigrants can access green-collar jobs.

In New York, Sustainable South Bronx runs a program that teaches participants how to install green roofs, clean toxic spills and restore rivers. Of the 128 low-income workers who have completed the program, 85 percent currently have jobs. In California, Women's

Green jobs can be found in existing industries. Wind turbines, like these, provide a need for architects, engineers, and other skilled professionals.

Action to Gain Economic Security has helped low-income immigrant women build four successful green housecleaning cooperatives that employ hundreds. And in Chicago, Growing Home has trained 100 formerly incarcerated, homeless or addicted individuals in organic farming. Sixty-five program graduates are now employed, and 90 have found permanent housing.

In 2008, similar training programs opened in Los Angeles, Newark and Oakland. Obama has also pledged to expand federal job-training programs to include green skills.

But for all its promise, the green economy offers no guarantees of justice for workers. Campaigns to raise wages, to improve benefits and to unify labor will remain as important in the green future as they are in the present.

EVALUATING THE AUTHOR'S ARGUMENTS:

The author quotes a study as well as an author in his article. Does this strengthen his argument? Why or why not?

Viewpoint

4

Green Jobs Will Not Be the Salvation of the Economy

"The . . . 'green jobs' agenda now being promoted in the U.S. in fact destroys jobs."

Tony Blankley

In the following essay Tony Blankley argues that a government-subsidized "green jobs agenda" is bad for the economy. He cites a Spanish university study that found that green jobs cost taxpayers extra money, raise energy costs, and create more job losses than job gains. A subsidized green economy makes sense if the goal is stopping global warming, he writes, but it is not an efficient way to create jobs. Blankley is a conservative writer and appears on the syndicated public radio show *Left, Right & Center.*

AS YOU READ, CONSIDER THE FOLLOWING QUESTIONS:

1. What percentage of green jobs created were permanent jobs operating and maintaining renewable sources of energy, according to the study cited by the author?
2. What was the average subsidy for each green job, according to the study?
3. How much higher was the cost of renewable energy over carbon-based energy between 2000 and 2008, according to the study?

Tony Blankley, "The Myth of 5 Million Green Jobs," *Real Clear Politics,* May 27, 2009. Reproduced by permission of Tony Blankley and Creators Syndicate, Inc.

In 1845, the French economist Frederic Bastiat published a satirical petition from the "Manufacturers of Candles" to the French Chamber of Deputies, which ridiculed the arguments made on behalf of inefficient industries to protect them from more efficient producers:

> "We are suffering from the ruinous competition of a rival who apparently works under conditions so far superior to our own for the production of light that he is flooding the domestic market with it at an incredibly low price; for the moment he appears, our sales cease, all the consumers turn to him, and a branch of French industry whose ramifications are innumerable is all at once reduced to complete stagnation. This rival, which is none other than the sun, is waging war on us. . . We ask you to be so good as to pass a law requiring the closing of all windows, dormers, skylights, inside and outside shutters, curtains, casements, bull's-eyes, deadlights, and blinds—in short, all openings, holes, chinks, and fissures through which the light of the sun is wont to enter houses, to the detriment of the fair industries with which, we are proud to say, we have endowed the country."

The author cites a Spanish study that showed that the creation of "green jobs" caused shut-downs and loss of jobs in other areas of the economy. The Spanish study found that approximately 2.2 other jobs would be lost for every green job created.

This famous put-down highlights the problem of claiming that protecting inefficient producers creates good jobs. Obviously, the money the French would have wasted on unneeded candles could have been spent on needed products and services—to the increased prosperity of the French economy.

I mention this in the context of the Obama administration's assertion that by subsidizing alternative energy sources, it will create 5 million green jobs. To that end, Congress passed in the stimulus bill $110 billion to subsidize and otherwise support such green efforts. And in conceptual support of that argument, the administration has referred to "what's happening in countries like Spain, Germany and Japan, where they're making real investments in renewable energy."

Well, in March [2009], one of Spain's leading universities, Universidad Rey Juan Carlos, published an authoritative study "of the effects on employment of public aid to renewable energy sources." The report pointed out: "This study is important for several reasons. First is that the Spanish experience is considered a leading example to be followed by many policy advocates and politicians. This study marks the very first time a critical analysis of the actual performance and impact has been made. Most important, it demonstrates that the Spanish/EU-style 'green jobs' agenda now being promoted in the U.S. in fact destroys jobs, detailing this in terms of jobs destroyed per job created."

More Jobs Lost than Created

The central finding of the study is that—treating the data optimistically— for every renewable-energy job that the government finances, "Spain's experience reveals with high confidence, by two different methods, that the U.S. should expect a loss of at least 2.2 jobs on average, or about 9 jobs lost for every 4 created."

Despite expensive and extensive green-job policies, a surprisingly low number of jobs were created. And about two-thirds of those

"Choices," cartoon by Ed Fischer, www.CartoonStock.com. Copyright © Ed Fischer. Reproduction rights obtainable from www.CartoonStock.com.

"green" jobs were just to set up the energy source, in construction, fabrication, installation, marketing and administration. Only 10 percent of the green jobs created were permanent jobs actually operating and maintaining the renewable sources of energy.

Each wind industry job created in Spain required a subsidy of about $1.4 million. Overall, the average subsidy cost for each green job was about $800,000 (571,138 euros). And to create about 50,000 green jobs, Spain lost 110,000 jobs elsewhere in the economy, principally in metallurgy, nonmetallic mining and food processing and in the beverage and tobacco industries.

Each green megawatt brought on line destroyed 5.28 jobs elsewhere in the economy (8.99 by photovoltaics, 4.27 by wind energy and 5.05 by mini-hydropower). The total higher energy cost—the higher cost of renewable energy over the market price of carbon-based energy—between 2000 and 2008 was about $10 billion. Moreover, the report concluded, "These costs do not appear to be unique to Spain's approach but instead are largely inherent in schemes to promote renewable energy sources."

An Enormous Cost

The high cost of green energy predictably drove energy-intensive Spanish companies and industries out of Spain to countries with cheaper carbon-based energy, while the cost to Spanish taxpayers of renewable-energy subsidies was "enormous—4.35 percent of all (value-added taxes) collected, 3.45 percent of the household income tax, or 5.6 percent of the corporate income tax."

There is much more in the report, which at about 50 pages in length would make useful reading for our elected representatives. Those who are worried about global warming may, after studying this report, still want to subsidize renewable-energy production. But it will be hard for such people to honestly continue to believe that they can think they are addressing global warming while creating millions of net new jobs.

EVALUATING THE AUTHOR'S ARGUMENTS:

Blankley describes the study he cites as "authoritative" and Universidad Rey Juan Carlos as "one of Spain's leading universities" but does not provide any data to back up his assertions. Do you see this as problematic in his argument or not? Why or why not?

Credit Card Reform Is Good for the Economy

"The new CARD Act reforms start restoring balance to our financial system so that it works for the best interests of America's families and America's economy once again."

Jeff Merkley

In the following selection U.S. senator Jeff Merkley argues that the 2009 Credit Card Accountability, Responsibility and Disclosure Act, or CARD Act, is in the best interests of the economy and America's families. For too long, he writes, unregulated consumer credit practices have been stripping wealth from families, and the CARD Act is a good first step to creating a fairer system. He also argues for a strong Consumer Financial Protection Agency that would offer ongoing oversight of the credit industry to prevent future abuses of the system. Merkley is a U.S. senator from Oregon.

Jeff Merkley, "Credit Card Reform Helps Economy," *StatesmanJournal.com,* August 30, 2009.

AS YOU READ, CONSIDER THE FOLLOWING QUESTIONS:
1. Name two provisions of the part of the CARD Act that went into effect in August 2009, according to the author.
2. List two parts of the CARD Act that went into effect in February 2010, according to the article.
3. According to the author, the country does well when who does well?

I magine signing a contract with a bank for a loan, but the bank is allowed to increase your interest rate at any time for any reason, charge you late fees even if your payment is on time and divert payments away from high interest balances so that you can never really pay off the loan.

Most folks would tell the bank, "No thanks." But of course, almost all of us already have one of these deals—it's called a credit card.

Credit cards can be useful tools, providing us with payment convenience and revolving credit when we need it. However, banks have written the rules to strip wealth from working families, utilizing all sorts of tricky bait and switch tactics, exploding interest rates and outrageous fees.

That is now changing.

Earlier this year [2009], Congress passed and the president signed the Credit Card Accountability, Responsibility and Disclosure Act, or CARD Act. This first-of-its-kind bill—which I was pleased to help pass out of committee on a 12–11 vote—finally places some common-sense limits on what credit card companies can do.

Fast Fact

Almost three in four people surveyed by CreditCards.com say they do not bother reading the terms and conditions of their credit cards.

The Changes

Starting this month [August 2009], credit card companies will have to send your bill 21 days in advance to make sure you have enough time to receive it and send back payment. They will have to give you

45 days notice before changing the terms of your agreement so that you can decide whether or not you want to keep that card. And the banks now won't be able to unilaterally charge you more for money you already borrowed: They will have to give you the option of closing your account and paying off the balance at the existing rate.

The rest of the CARD Act will go into effect in February 2010. At that point, banks will be barred from arbitrarily increasing the interest rate on money you have already borrowed without requiring you to close your account. They will also periodically have to evaluate your account to determine whether you qualify for a reduction in rates. Also going into effect includes a ban on multiple over-the-limit fees during a single billing cycle, a requirement that payments be applied first to the balance with the highest interest rate and limits on aggressive marketing to young people.

Ensuring a Fair Financial Marketplace

This law starts leveling the playing field between consumers and powerful financial institutions, but there is much more we can and should do to ensure fairness throughout the financial marketplace. Most

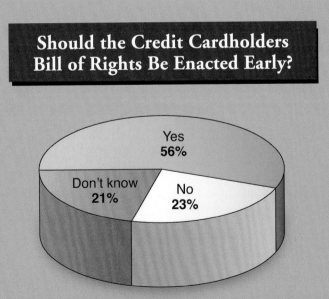

Should the Credit Cardholders Bill of Rights Be Enacted Early?

Yes 56%

Don't know 21%

No 23%

*The Credit Cardholders Bill of Rights was the original name of the bill that became the CARD Act.

Taken from: GfK Custom Research and Credit.com, October 14, 2009.

On May 20, 2009, U.S. House members Dan Maffei (D-NY), Carolyn Maloney (D-NY), Keith Ellison (D-MN), and Walter Jones (R-NC) discuss the passing of the credit card reform bill, also called Credit Cardholders Bill of Rights, by the House of Representatives.

importantly, we must move quickly to create a strong Consumer Financial Protection Agency. This new agency would ensure that we have the ongoing, professional oversight of our consumer credit markets to prevent the proliferation of new tricks and traps. We shouldn't need landmark legislation like the CARD Act every time the financial industry thinks up new practices that are clearly abusive.

Our country does well when middle-class Americans do well. But for too long, unregulated consumer credit practices have been stripping wealth from our families, turning a useful tool into a destructive force. The new CARD Act reforms start restoring balance to our financial system so that it works for the best interests of America's families and America's economy once again.

EVALUATING THE AUTHOR'S ARGUMENTS:

The author of the article is a Democratic U.S. senator. What effect, if any, do you think this has on how you read his argument?

Credit Cards Keep Americans in a "Buy Now, Pay Later" Mentality

Ellen Ruppel Shell

"When it comes to credit cards, is raising the price of entry and ownership really such a bad thing?"

The 2009 Credit Card Accountability, Responsibility and Disclosure Act, or CARD Act, makes credit cards harder to get and raises introductory rates and fees—and that is a good thing, argues Ellen Ruppel Shell in the following selection. For too long, she argues, cheap credit has lured Americans into mortgaging their futures for the thrill of immediate gratification. Americans' resulting credit problems, she writes, are not just the fault of predatory lending companies but also consumers willing to sign up for "unbeatable" credit offers. Shell is a contributing editor to the *Atlantic* and the author of *Cheap: The High Price of Discount Culture.*

Ellen Ruppel Shell, "The High Cost of Cheap Credit," *The Boston Globe*, June 7, 2009. Reproduced by permission of the author.

AS YOU READ, CONSIDER THE FOLLOWING QUESTIONS:

1. How many high school seniors use credit cards, according to the author?
2. What percentage of college students graduate free of credit card debt, according to the author?
3. What is the percentage of people who were offered new credit in the first year after they declared bankruptcy, according to a University of Iowa study cited by the author?

The new credit card law has been widely hailed as a David vs. Goliath victory of hapless consumers over venal lenders. "People can feel a lot more comfortable about the rules of the game," Adam Levin, chairman and founder of Credit.com, told the Associated Press. "But there will be some fallout, and it might be a short-term negative."

Among the negatives Levin cites are higher introductory rates and fees. But when it comes to credit cards, is raising the price of entry and ownership really such a bad thing? You don't need a credit history or even a job to get a credit card. Kids typically get their first solicitations in high school—one out of three high school seniors use them, and half of those carry cards in their own name. Seventy-eight percent of college students have credit cards, and, according to student loan maker Nellie Mae, typically carry a balance of $3,200. One out of 10 college students is more than $7,800 in the hole to at least one credit card company, and only 19 percent manage to graduate free of credit card debt. Yes, students and easy credit can be a dangerous combination, but not necessarily the most dangerous. That would be easy credit and the bankrupt.

Fast Fact

There were 309 million Visa credit cards and 211 million MasterCard credit cards in circulation in the United States in 2009.

In a shocking study titled "Bankrupt Profits: The Credit Industry's Business Model for Postbankruptcy Lending," Katherine Porter of the University of Iowa found that 96 percent of those polled were offered new credit in the first year after they declared bankruptcy. Porter concludes: "The modern credit industry sees bankrupt families as lucrative targets for high-yield lending, a reality that has important implications for developing optimal consumer credit policy and bankruptcy law."

Lucrative targets, yes, but whose fault is that? Surely some of the blame must fall on consumers willing to take lenders up on these "unbeatable" offers. Over the past 18 months or so, thousands of foreclosures and bankruptcies have made clear that what seems like cheap credit is anything but a bargain. Cheap mortgages led us to believe that we could afford to pay more for a home than we should, with the promise that when we run out of money we can just "take it out of the house" in yet another "easy" mortgage. When we maxed out one credit card, we just pulled out another one—after all, they were "free."

High school seniors use credit cards, and it has been noted that 78 percent of all college students use credit cards.

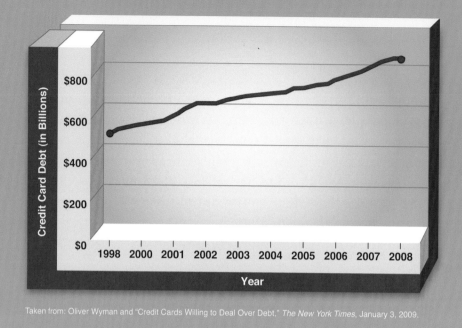

Outstanding Credit Card Debt in the United States

Credit Card Debt (in Billions)

$800
$600
$400
$200
$0

1998 2000 2001 2002 2003 2004 2005 2006 2007 2008

Year

Taken from: Oliver Wyman and "Credit Cards Willing to Deal Over Debt," *The New York Times*, January 3, 2009.

Cheap Credit Has a Steep Price

Cheap credit disassociates our wants from our needs, distances the thrill of ownership from the kill-joy vexation of having to pay for it. But credit is a tool like any other—a chain saw comes to mind—that is extremely useful when used with knowledge and forethought, but extremely dangerous if used capriciously. The siren call of "low, low introductory prices" can mislead us, not only in the case of credit, but in many things.

Cheap loans, cheap goods, cheap food all exact a price. In the long run, many of us pay through the nose for all those incredible "bargains," not only with our credit ratings, but with our health, freedom, and even our futures. Freshly minted college grads chin-deep in debt have little choice but to grab whatever job they can, regardless of its long-term prospects, or its relationship to their interests and goals. Home "owners" who bought into "no money down, low-interest" balloon mortgages discover too late that they not only do not own their home, but that the bank owns them.

Bargain hunting is a time-honored tradition, and that's not going to change, nor should it. But psychologists agree that the "thrill" of bagging a great deal is frequently followed by deep regret and disappointment. It's time to put the false era of "something for next to nothing" behind us, to stop paying for our future on the no-money-down "installment" plan.

The power to enact change resides not only in the voting booth, but in our wallets. The first step is to recognize that our purchasing decisions have consequences that go well beyond the immediate deal at hand, and that over time a low price of entry can exact extraordinary long-term costs.

As individuals and as a nation, it's time to rethink our "buy now, pay later" mentality, secure in the knowledge that real value has never been and never will be cheap.

EVALUATING THE AUTHOR'S ARGUMENTS:

Shell expands her argument against cheap credit to cheap goods and cheap foods as well. Do you think this enhances her argument or dilutes it? Explain.

Capitalism Is the Best System for the Future

George W. Bush

> *"[Capitalism] is by far the most efficient and just way of structuring an economy."*

In the following viewpoint, excerpted from a speech then-president George W. Bush delivered at the Federal Hall National Memorial in 2008, he argues that despite crises in the U.S. economy, free market capitalism is still the best system for promoting prosperity. The free market system, he says, provides the incentives that lead to prosperity—the incentive to work, to innovate, to save, to invest wisely, and to create jobs for others. When everyone is part of such a system, he argues, the society as a whole benefits.

AS YOU READ, CONSIDER THE FOLLOWING QUESTIONS:

1. In this speech the former president lists four reforms to strengthen the global economy. List two of them.
2. Name two countries that, according to the speech, benefited from the free market system.
3. List two examples of countries that experienced "devastating results" from a non–free market system, according to the speech.

George W. Bush, "President Bush Discusses Financial Markets and World Economy, Federal Hall National Memorial, New York, New York," in *The White House,* Office of the Press Secretary, November 13, 2008.

Ｗe live in a world in which our economies are interconnected. Prosperity and progress have reached farther than any time in our history. Unfortunately, as we have seen in recent months, financial turmoil anywhere in the world affects economies everywhere in the world. And so this weekend I'm going to host a Summit on Financial Markets and the World Economy with leaders from developed and developing nations that account for nearly 90 percent of the world economy. . .

It will focus on five key objectives: understanding the causes of the global crisis, reviewing the effectiveness of our responses thus far, developing principles for reforming our financial and regulatory systems, launching a specific action plan to implement those principles, and reaffirming our conviction that free market principles offer the surest path to lasting prosperity. (Applause.)

First, we're working toward a common understanding of the causes behind the global crisis. Different countries will naturally bring different perspectives, but there are some points on which we can all agree:

Over the past decade, the world experienced a period of strong economic growth. Nations accumulated huge amounts of savings, and looked for safe places to invest them. Because of our attractive political, legal, and entrepreneurial climates, the United States and other developed nations received a large share of that money.

The massive inflow of foreign capital, combined with low interest rates, produced a period of easy credit. And that easy credit especially affected the housing market. Flush with cash, many lenders issued mortgages and many borrowers could not afford them. Financial institutions then purchased these loans, packaged them together, and converted them into complex securities designed to yield large returns. These securities were then purchased by investors and financial institutions in the United States and Europe and elsewhere—often with little analysis of their true underlying value.

The financial crisis was ignited when booming housing markets began to decline. As home values dropped, many borrowers defaulted on their mortgages, and institutions holding securities backed by those mortgages suffered serious losses. Because of outdated regulatory structures and poor risk management practices, many financial institutions in America and Europe were too highly leveraged. When capital ran short, many faced severe financial jeopardy. This led to high-profile failures of financial institutions in America and Europe, led to contractions and widespread anxiety—all of which contributed to sharp declines in the equity markets.

The United States Is Taking the Right Steps

These developments have placed a heavy burden on hardworking people around the world. Stock market drops have eroded the value of retirement accounts and pension funds. The tightening of credit has made it harder for families to borrow money for cars or home improvements or education of the children. Businesses have found it harder to get loans to expand their operations and create jobs. Many nations have suffered job losses, and have serious concerns about the worsening economy. Developing nations have been hit hard as nervous investors have withdrawn their capital.

We are faced with the prospect of a global meltdown. And so we've responded with bold measures. I'm a market-oriented guy, but not when I'm faced with the prospect of a global meltdown. At Saturday's summit, we're going to review the effectiveness of our actions.

Here in the United States, we have taken unprecedented steps to boost liquidity, recapitalize financial institutions, guarantee most new debt issued by insured banks, and prevent the disorderly collapse of large, interconnected enterprises. These were historic actions taken necessary to make—necessary so that the economy would not melt down and affect millions of our fellow citizens. . . .

This crisis did not develop overnight, and it's not going to be solved overnight. But our actions are having an impact. Credit markets are beginning to thaw. Businesses are gaining access to essential short-term financing. A measure of stability is returning to financial systems here at home and around the world. It's going to require more time for these improvements to fully take hold, and there's going to be difficult days ahead. But the United States and our partners are taking the right steps to get through this crisis.

Broader Reforms Are Needed

In addition to addressing the current crisis, we will also need to make broader reforms to strengthen the global economy over the long term.

American Attitudes Toward Capitalism Compared to Other Countries

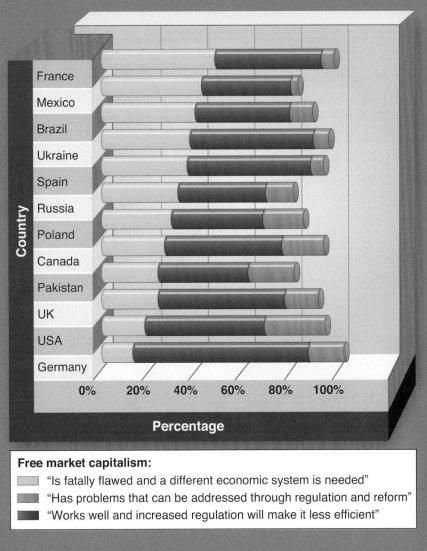

Country (vertical axis):
France, Mexico, Brazil, Ukraine, Spain, Russia, Poland, Canada, Pakistan, UK, USA, Germany

Percentage (horizontal axis): 0%, 20%, 40%, 60%, 80%, 100%

Free market capitalism:

- "Is fatally flawed and a different economic system is needed"
- "Has problems that can be addressed through regulation and reform"
- "Works well and increased regulation will make it less efficient"

Taken from: Globescan poll for BBC World Service, November 9, 2009.

This weekend, leaders will establish principles for adapting our financial systems to the realities of the 21st century marketplace. We will discuss specific actions we can take to implement these principles. We will direct our finance ministers to work with other experts and report back to us with detailed recommendations on further reasonable actions.

One vital principle of reform is that our nations must make our financial markets more transparent. For example, we should consider improving accounting rules for securities, so that investors around the world can understand the true value of the assets they purchase.

Secondly, we must ensure that markets, firms, and financial products are properly regulated. For example, credit default swaps—financial products that insure against potential losses—should be processed through centralized clearinghouses instead of through unregulated, "over the counter" markets. By bringing greater stability to this large and important financial sector, we reduce the risk to our overall financial systems.

Third, we must enhance the integrity of our financial markets. For example, authorities in every nation should take a fresh look at the rules governing market manipulation and fraud—and ensure that investors are properly protected.

Fourth, we must strengthen cooperation among the world's financial authorities. For example, leading nations should better coordinate national laws and regulations. We should also reform international financial institutions such as the IMF and the World Bank, which are based largely on the economic order of 1944. To better reflect the realities of today's global economy, both the IMF and World Bank should modernize their governance structures. They should consider extending greater voter—voting power to dynamic developing nations, especially as they increase their contributions to these institutions. They should consider ways to streamline their executive boards, and make them more representative.

In addition to these important—to these management changes, we should move forward with other reforms to make the IMF and World Bank more transparent, accountable, and effective. For example, the IMF should agree to work more closely with member countries to ensure that their exchange rate policies are market-oriented and fair. And the World Bank should ensure its development programs reflect the priorities of the people they are designed to serve—and focus on measurable results.

All these steps require decisive actions from governments around the world. At the same time, we must recognize that government intervention is not a cure-all. For example, some blame the crisis on insufficient regulation of the American mortgage market. But many European countries had much more extensive regulations, and still experienced problems almost identical to our own.

History has shown that the greater threat to economic prosperity is not too little government involvement in the market, it is too much government involvement in the market. (Applause.) We saw this in the case of Fannie Mae and Freddie Mac. Because these firms were chartered by the United States Congress, many believed they were backed by the full faith and credit of the United States government. Investors put huge amounts of money into Fannie and Freddie, which they used to build up irresponsibly large portfolios of mortgage-backed securities. And when the housing market declined, these securities, of course, plummeted in value. It took a taxpayer-funded rescue to keep Fannie and Freddie from collapsing in a way that would have devastated the global financial system. And there is a clear lesson: Our aim should not be more government—it should be smarter government.

All this leads to the most important principle that should guide our work: While reforms in the financial sector are essential, the long-term solution to today's problems is sustained economic growth. And the surest path to that growth is free markets and free people. (Applause.)

Capitalism Is "the Engine of Social Mobility"

This is a decisive moment for the global economy. In the wake of the financial crisis, voices from the left and right are equating the free enterprise system with greed and exploitation and failure. It's true this crisis included failures—by lenders and borrowers and by financial firms and by governments and independent regulators. But the crisis was not a failure of the free market system. And the answer is not to try to reinvent that system. It is to fix the problems we face, make the reforms we need, and move forward with the free market principles that have delivered prosperity and hope to people all across the globe.

Like any other system designed by man, capitalism is not perfect. It can be subject to excesses and abuse. But it is by far the most efficient and just way of structuring an economy. At its most basic level, capitalism offers people the freedom to choose where they work and what they do, the opportunity to buy or sell products they want, and the dignity that comes with profiting from their talent and hard work. The free market system provides the incentives that lead to prosperity—the incentive to work, to innovate, to save, to invest wisely, and to create jobs for others. And as millions of people pursue these incentives together, whole societies benefit.

Free market capitalism is far more than economic theory. It is the engine of social mobility—the highway to the American Dream. It's what makes it possible for a husband and wife to start their own business, or a new immigrant to open a restaurant, or a single mom to go back to college and to build a better career. It is what allowed entrepreneurs in Silicon Valley to change the way the world sells products and searches for information. It's what transformed America from a rugged frontier to the greatest economic power in history—a nation that gave the world the steamboat and the airplane, the computer and the CAT scan, the Internet and the iPod.

Ultimately, the best evidence for free market capitalism is its performance compared to other economic systems. Free markets allowed Japan, an island with few natural resources, to recover from war and grow into the world's second-largest economy. Free markets allowed South Korea to make itself into one of the most technologically advanced societies in the world. Free markets turned small areas like Singapore and Hong Kong and Taiwan into global economic players. Today, the success of the world's largest economies comes from their embrace of free markets.

Meanwhile, nations that have pursued other models have experienced devastating results. Soviet communism starved millions, bankrupted an empire, and collapsed as decisively as the Berlin Wall. Cuba, once known for its vast fields of cane, is now forced to ration sugar. And while Iran sits atop giant oil reserves, its people cannot put enough gasoline in its—in their cars.

On May 13, 2009, Senator Christopher Dodd (D-CT), Chair of the Senate Banking Committee, waits to speak to a conference about credit card fees and financial regulation. The author of the viewpoint asserts that capitalism may need some fixes, such as more regulation, transparency, and accountability, but should not be replaced.

The record is unmistakable: If you seek economic growth, if you seek opportunity, if you seek social justice and human dignity, the free market system is the way to go. (Applause.) And it would be a terrible mistake to allow a few months of crisis to undermine 60 years of success.

Free Trade Is a Key Component of Capitalism

Just as important as maintaining free markets within countries is maintaining the free movement of goods and services between countries. When nations open their markets to trade and investment, their businesses and farmers and workers find new buyers for their products. Consumers benefit from more choices and better prices. Entrepreneurs can get their ideas off the ground with funding from anywhere in the world. Thanks in large part to open markets, the volume of global trade today is nearly 30 times greater than it was six decades ago—and some of the most dramatic gains have come in the developing world.

As President, I have seen the transformative power of trade up close. I've been to a Caterpillar factory in East Peoria, Illinois, where thousands of good-paying American jobs are supported by exports. I've walked the grounds of a trade fair in Ghana, where I met women who support their families by exporting handmade dresses and jewelry. I've spoken with a farmer in Guatemala who decided to grow high-value crops he could sell overseas—and helped create more than 1,000 jobs.

Stories like these show why it is so important to keep markets open to trade and investment. This openness is especially urgent during times of economic strain. Shortly after the stock market crash in 1929, Congress passed the Smoot-Hawley tariff—a protectionist measure designed to wall off America's economy from global competition. The result was not economic security. It was economic ruin. And leaders around the world must keep this example in mind, and reject the temptation of protectionism. (Applause.)

Capitalism Will Lift America Out of Crisis

There are clear-cut ways for nations to demonstrate the commitment to open markets. The United States Congress has an immediate opportunity by approving free trade agreements with Colombia, Peru, and South Korea. America and other wealthy nations must also ensure this crisis does not become an excuse to reverse our engagement with the developing world. And developing nations should continue policies that foster enterprise and investment. As well, all nations should pledge to conclude a framework this year that leads to a successful Doha agreement.

We're facing this challenge together and we're going to get through it together. The United States is determined to show the way back to economic growth and prosperity. I know some may question whether America's leadership in the global economy will continue. The world can be confident that it will, because our markets are flexible and we can rebound from setbacks. We saw that resilience in the 1940s, when America pulled itself out of Depression, marshaled a powerful army, and helped save the world from tyranny. We saw that resilience in the 1980s, when Americans overcame gas lines, turned stagflation into strong economic growth, and won the Cold War. We saw that resilience after September the 11th, 2001, when our nation recovered from a brutal attack, revitalized our shaken economy, and rallied the forces of freedom in the great ideological struggle of the 21st century.

The world will see the resilience of America once again. We will work with our partners to correct the problems in the global financial system. We will rebuild our economic strength. And we will continue to lead the world toward prosperity and peace.

Thanks for coming and God bless. (Applause.)

EVALUATING THE AUTHOR'S ARGUMENTS:

George W. Bush was a polarizing figure in American politics. Did you have any preconceived notions as you began this piece? And, if so, did they change after reading it?

The United States Needs to Move Beyond Capitalism

"[The death of capitalism is] the opportunity of a lifetime . . . the opportunity to stop using what no longer works and figure out what does."

Steven G. Brant

For Steven G. Brant, the government bailout of A.I.G. in 2008 was final confirmation of the death of capitalism. Capitalism, he argues, is a system based on rules that applied in the past and that the conditions that the rules were based on are no longer true. But instead of mourning the death of capitalism, we can look at it as an opportunity, writes Brant. It is an opportunity for talented designers to develop a "New Economy" based on principles that will work in today's world. Brant is a researcher, theorist, and developer of sustainable development strategies.

AS YOU READ, CONSIDER THE FOLLOWING QUESTIONS:

1. Why, according to the author, should the government have let A.I.G. fail?
2. What does the author describe as a "clean sheet of paper" approach?
3. What, according to the author, does a new economic system need to be based on?

C apitalism is dead. And I'm not surprised. "I'll explain why in a minute, but first here's Capitalism's obituary. It's the *New York Times'* lead story on the bailout of A.I.G. . . .

WASHINGTON—Fearing a financial crisis worldwide, the Federal Reserve reversed course on Tuesday and agreed to an $85 billion bailout that would give the government control of the troubled insurance giant American International Group.

The decision, only two weeks after the Treasury took over the federally chartered mortgage finance companies Fannie Mae and Freddie Mac, is the most radical intervention in private business in the central bank's history.

With time running out after A.I.G. failed to get a bank loan to avoid bankruptcy, Treasury Secretary Henry M. Paulson Jr. and the Fed chairman, Ben S. Bernanke, convened a meeting with House and Senate leaders on Capitol Hill about 6:30 p.m. Tuesday to explain the rescue plan. They emerged just after 7:30 p.m. with Mr. Paulson and Mr. Bernanke looking grim, but with top lawmakers initially expressing support for the plan. But the bailout is likely to prove controversial, because it effectively puts taxpayer money at risk while protecting bad investments made by A.I.G. and other institutions it does business with.

Hmm . . . ". . . the bailout is likely to prove controversial, because it effectively puts taxpayer money at risk while protecting bad investments made by A.I.G. and other institutions it does business with."
Controversial? No. Not to me. Confirmational. That's what it is.
It confirms that our nation is not willing to let Capitalism be Capitalism, except for us little guys of course. But here's the thing. If Capitalism isn't Capitalism for the Big Guys, then it isn't Capitalism for the little guys either.
Just like there's no such thing as being a little bit pregnant, there's no such thing as having a little Capitalism over here and a little Socialism over there. You can't have two economic systems operating in one country at the same time, at least not if "all men are created equal" is written in that country's founding documents. Sorry, my friends. You either have Capitalism or you don't. And here in the USA, we no longer have it. It's dead.

Think about this. Our government has just decided—without asking any of us, including our Congressional representatives—that $85 billion more of our money should be used to cover the actions of (and pardon the unsophisticated language here) stupid, greedy, criminal people. Stupid, because they didn't have a clue that what they were doing would have such negative consequences. Greedy, because all they could see were short term dollar signs in front of their eyes. Criminal, because they just robbed you and me of $85 billion dollars by holding a "we're too big to fail" gun to the head of the US government.

The System Is Failed

They should have let A.I.G. fail, because—if that had brought about the collapse of the global economic system—that would have just sped up our journey to a point of systemic collapse we are destined to reach anyway. I say destined to reach not because it's God's will but because no system can continue to function when its fundamental design is flawed. You see, the current global economic system is based on a fundamental assumption that—while it was true when the system was first set up—is no longer true today.

Let me give you another way of thinking about this. If a car that is designed to handle any road condition at any speed suddenly finds itself traveling across the water, it will quickly sink below the surface even as its wheels keep spinning. And, if the driver remains oblivious to the fact that there's no longer a road under his or her car, that driver will die.

We are no longer on land, my friends. We are in a car when we should be in a boat (or maybe an airplane). The global reality has shifted, but our political leaders are largely blind to this reality. They think we're still on dry land.

More about all this in a minute. But first, back to the US economy.
. . .

Socialism Is Already Here

The funny thing is, I've known that a significant portion of the US economy is Socialistic for years. "What are you talking about?", you ask. "The Military Industrial Complex," I answer.

You do know that all military weapons are purchased using "cost plus" contracts, in which businesses are guaranteed a profit, don't you? And that literally every weapons system comes in over its original budget . . . and that those cost overruns are absorbed by the government, not the arms manufacturer? There is no Capitalism in the Military Industrial Complex. It's all Socialism, justified by the concept that these weapons are so important to American security that the companies that manufacture them have to be guaranteed a profit, so they don't accidentally go out of business. (By the way, I worked in contracting years ago at the Army Corps of Engineers. So, I know something about how military contracts work.)

> ## Fast Fact
>
> In a 2009 CBS poll 53 percent of Americans said they disapproved of the government providing money to banks and financial institutions, 37 percent said they approved.

Now, getting back to the death of Capitalism in America as a whole, don't be so sad. You know the expression: "From every emergency, there's a chance for something new to emerge"? Well, that's where we are. We are in one hell of an emergency. And—if you'll step back for a minute—you'll see it's the opportunity of a lifetime . . . the opportunity to stop using what no longer works and figure out what does.

And now I'm going to surprise you by (partially) agreeing with John McCain. He says we need a Commission to study the problem. And I agree. But we don't need a Commission of the kind John McCain suggests we have. His Commission would consist of financial experts. And that won't do. Because financial experts are experts in the past.

We need to bring specific, outside of Washington expertise to the party. But they must be experts in the future, not the past.

Starting from Scratch

And what kind of people are experts in the future? Designers. That's what kind.

Designers know how to envision what's possible from the best of what we know how to do today. They know how to take a *clean*

The viewpoint author asserts that the $85 billion bailout of American International Group (AIG) is a sign of mixing capitalism with socialism and so is a sign that capitalism has failed and should be replaced.

sheet of paper approach to figuring out how to fulfill a particular need. Designers know how to take a system that no longer works . . . determine what assumptions (or design principles) used to build the system are still correct and which are incorrect . . . substitute new assumptions or principles where necessary . . . and develop and implement a new design appropriate to the reality of today.

We need people like that . . . people who know that a tipping point has been reached . . . that the ground on which our old economic system has stood has disappeared . . . and that, as a result, the old system is totally dysfunctional. But at the same time, these experts must know how functional—how *elegantly functional*—our new economic system can be!

We have a chance for something new . . . something beautiful . . . to emerge from this emergency! But to do this, we need people who understand how to take a culture through a Great Transition . . . a transition based on recognizing we're no longer on dry land, as I mentioned above.

So, if we are no longer on dry land, where are we?

Scarcity Has Been Replaced by Abundance

Well, the "dry land" of the past is the zero-sum, fixed pie, scarcity of resources based economic model that has existed since the beginning . . . since the time when two groups of cave dwellers fought over a watering hole that contained enough water for only one group to survive. Humanity has been on that "dry land" for a long, long time. But science and technology—including the power to capture limitless amounts of energy from the Sun—has progressed to the point where we can live in a society based on an economic system based on abundance (not scarcity).

A world where it's possible for all survival needs to be met. That's where we live now. Call it water or air, it's definitely not the dry land of the past.

And that's why Capitalism has died. Because it is a system that is compelled to try and make more and more money based on Darwinian principles that are no longer true. They were true when Capitalism was created, but they are obsolete now. This death was inevitable, because the mismatch between the world Wall Street thinks exists and the world that really exists is so fundamentals . . . the methods needed to continue making money in a world of the past had become so complicated . . . that self destruction was only a matter of time.

If the universe is a giant clock, you can only last for so long if you don't work the machinery the way it's designed to work. You will blow up the clock if you don't change what you're doing. . . .

Thanks to the death of Capitalism, that adventure is an idea whose time has come. Let's look for leaders who understand the need to figure out how to live in this new world. Leaders like Barack Obama. And leaders (hopefully) like the person you see in the mirror every morning.

EVALUATING THE AUTHOR'S ARGUMENTS:

In this argument, did Brant convince you that developing a new economic system would be a good idea? Why or why not?

Facts About the U.S. Economy

Editor's note: These facts can be used in reports or papers to reinforce or add credibility when making important points or claims.

The U.S. Economy at a Glance

- The United States has the largest economy in the world. The economy in California alone is so large that, if it were a country, it would be ranked among the top ten biggest economies in the world.
- The 2009 Gross Domestic Product (GDP, the total value of goods and services produced) was estimated to be $14.2 trillion.
- The average hourly wage in the United States as of January 2010 was $22.45, according to the Bureau of Labor Statistics.
- The federal minimum wage (the lowest wage an employer can legally pay an employee) is $7.25 per hour.
- The unemployment rate in January 2010 was 9.7 percent.
- According to the 2009 poverty guidelines, a family of four earning less than $22,050 is considered to be living in poverty.
- Almost 40 million people in the United States were living in poverty in 2008, according to the most recent U.S. Census figures. The number equals 13.2 percent of the population.
- As of February 2009, the U.S. national debt was over $12 trillion. The average savings per citizen was a little over $1,000.

The Retail Sector

- Although chain stores have been around since 1859 when the first A&P grocery store opened in New York City, they did not become the dominant force in the retail world until the latter part of the twentieth century.
- Walmart is the world's largest retailer and had over $401 billion in sales for the fiscal year ending in January 2009.
- Walmart employs more than 1.4 million people in the United States, and it is one of the largest employers in the United States and Canada, and the largest employer in Mexico.

- 100 million Americans shop at Walmart each week at the more than 4,200 Walmart and Sam's Club stores in the United States.
- The total compensation for Mike Scott, the CEO of Walmart, in 2009 was $12,238,209.00, or about $5,883.75 an hour for a forty-hour work week. The average salary for a cashier at Walmart was about $8.45 an hour.
- Large retailers have been accused of contributing to or causing a host of societal problems, including lowered wages, the loss of locally owned small business, the weakening of unions, environmental degradation, more manufacturing jobs going overseas, the shifting of employee health care costs from businesses to government, decreased community atmosphere, urban sprawl, traffic, and inefficient land usage.
- Proponents of large retailers point to the megastores' success in selling affordable goods and providing jobs.
- In the fourth quarter of 2009, online retail sales reached $39 billion.
- The top three largest online retailers in 2009 were Amazon.com, Staples, and Dell.

The Global Financial Crisis
- The U.S. economy began to falter in 2007. The U.S. economic crisis contributed to what the International Monetary Fund termed "the deepest global recession since the Great Depression."
- Between 2007 and the end of 2009, the economic crisis caused over 5 million job losses.
- On September 29, 2008, the Dow Jones industrial average dropped nearly 778 points. The one-day drop caused the stock market to lose $1.2 trillion in value.
- Home values dropped $3.6 trillion in 2008. In the first 11 months of 2009, home values dropped $489 billion.
- The states with the highest foreclosure rates in 2009 were Nevada, Arizona, California, Florida, and Idaho. The rate of foreclosures in Las Vegas, the city with the highest rate, was five times the national average.
- As of February 2010, about 4 million homeowners nationwide were ninety days or more delinquent on their mortgages or in foreclosure proceedings.

- The Recovery Act, signed by President Obama on February 17, 2009, was designed to put $787 billion into the economy to create and save jobs.
- In January 2010, the Congressional Budget Office revised the cost of the Recovery Act to $862 billion.
- The Recovery Act monies enter the economy through tax cuts, entitlement programs, contracts, grants, and loans.
- In the last four months of 2009, the Recovery Act funded almost 600,000 jobs.
- The Recovery Act devoted more than $150 billion to public works programs to improve the infrastructure.
- In early 2010 a record 38 million people were enrolled in the assistance program for the hungry, funded by the act.
- Other government programs created to stimulate the economy included "Cash for Clunkers," a $3 billion program designed to encourage Americans to trade in old cars for new, fuel-efficent cars, and the $700 billion Troubled Asset Relief Program (TARP), which purchased troubled assets from banks and other financial companies.
- Other countries, including China, France, Germany, and Britain, also enacted stimulus programs during the crisis.

Glossary

budget deficit: Occurs when more money in the budget is spent than taken in.

capitalism: An economic system characterized by private ownership, letting the market determine prices with minimal government interference.

Credit Card Accountability, Responsibility, and Disclosure Act (the CARD Act): An act signed by President Obama in 2009 designed to protect consumers from unfair credit practices.

default on a loan: Not making payments on the loan.

foreclosure: The legal process in which a creditor takes over property when the mortgage holder is unable to pay.

401-(k) plan: A saving plan offered by corporations that allows employees to set aside tax-deferred income for retirement. Sometimes companies will match employee contributions to the account.

gross domestic product (GDP): An economic measure using the total market value of the goods and services produced in a given country.

International Monetary Fund (IMF): A United Nations organization responsible for stabilizing international exchange rates.

minimum wage: The lowest wage an employer can legally pay an employee.

SCHIP: The acronym for the State Children's Health Insurance Program—also known as Children's Health Insurance Program (CHIP)—a program that provides matching funds to states to provide health insurance for families with children. Qualifying families have low incomes but not low enough to qualify for Medicaid.

Organizations to Contact

The editors have compiled the following list of organizations concerned with the issues debated in this book. The descriptions are derived from materials provided by the organizations. All have publications or information available for interested readers. The list was compiled on the date of publication of the present volume; the information provided here may change. Be aware that many organizations take several weeks or longer to respond to inquiries, so allow as much time as possible for the receipt of requested materials.

Alliance for Health Care Reform
1444 Eye St. NW, Ste. 910
Washington, DC 20005
(202) 789-2300
fax: (202) 789-2233
e-mail: info@allhealth.org
Web site: www.allhealth.org/index.asp

Alliance for Health Care Reform is a nonpartisan, nonprofit group that believes that everyone in the United States should have health care at a reasonable cost. The alliance organizes forums with panels representing a balance of expert views, provides resources on health care issues to elected officials, and offers a media resource center to assist journalists working on health care issues. The alliance's Web site features information on health care issues, and the group produces regular issue briefs on topics such as "Rural Health and Health Reform" and "The Uninsured and Rising Health Costs."

American Enterprise Institute (AEI)
1150 Seventeenth St. NW
Washington, DC 20036
(202) 862-5800
fax: (202) 862-7177
e-mail: VRodman@aei.org
Web site: www.aei.org

AEI is a conservative, pro-business think tank dedicated to "expanding liberty, increasing individual opportunity, and strengthening free enterprise." Projects include the AEI Center for Regulatory and Market Studies and the Shadow Financial Regulatory Committee. The AEI Web site features the AEI *Outlook* and *On the Issues* series, which cover issues such as health policy and the financial crisis. AEI publishes the journal *The American*.

American Immigration Council
1331 G St. NW, Ste. 200
Washington, DC 20005-3141
(202) 507-7500
fax: (202) 742-5619
Web site: www.americanimmigrationcouncil.org

The American Immigration Council's stated mission is "honoring our immigrant past and shaping our immigrant future." The group works toward these goals through four key programs: Immigration Policy Center, Legal Action Center, International Exchange Center, and Community Education Center. The group issues several publications including *Special Reports, Immigrant Fact Checks*, and *Perspectives*.

The Center for Capitalism and Society
1134 International Affairs Building
420 West 118th St., Mail Code 3334
Columbia University
New York, NY 10027
(212) 851-0260
fax: (212) 851-5840
e-mail: kl2512@columbia.edu
Web site: http://capitalism.columbia.edu

The Center for Capitalism and Society seeks to analyze the factors that make an economy inclusive and dynamic. As part of this mission, the center organizes seminars, conferences, and media events to provide a forum for debate on the issues surrounding capitalism today. The center publishes the e-journal, *Capitalism & Society*.

The Jump$tart Coalition for Personal Financial Literacy
919 18th St. NW, Ste. 300
Washington, DC 20006
(888) 45-EDUCATE <888-453-3822>

fax: (202) 223-0321
e-mail: info@jumpstartcoalition.org
Web site: www.jumpstartcoalition.org

Jump$tart is a national coalition of organizations dedicated to improving the financial literacy of kindergarten through college-age youth by providing advocacy, research, standards, and educational resources. Jump$tart's Web site offers tools such as "The Reality Check" test designed to teach students what they will need to do to reach their financial goals. Jump$tart publishes the quarterly newsletter *Jump$tart Update*.

National Association of Consumer Advocates (NACA)
1730 Rhode Island Ave. NW, Ste. 710
Washington, DC 20036
(202) 452-1989
fax: (202) 452-0099
e-mail: info@naca.net
Web site: http://naca.net

NACA is a nonprofit association of consumer advocates and attorneys who work to protect consumers from fraudulent business practices. NACA promotes consumer rights by lobbying policy makers, drafting legislation, and advocating on behalf of consumers on a variety of issues including bankruptcy, predatory lending practices, and debt collection abuse. NACA publishes the *NACA Newsletter*.

National Endowment for Financial Education
5299 DTC Blvd., Ste. 1300
Greenwood Village, CO 80111
(303) 741-6333
fax: (303) 220-0838
Web site: www.nefe.org

The National Endowment for Financial Education is a national, nonprofit organization dedicated to improving the financial well-being of Americans. It offers a variety of services including materials for educators, research for consumers and think tanks, and free financial assistance to those who cannot afford a financial adviser. NEFE's High School Financial Planning Program includes a Web site, http://hsfpp .nefe.org/home, which has games, calculators, and articles for teens interested in financial issues. NEFE publishes the newsletter *NEFE Digest*.

National Foundation for Credit Counseling (NFCC)
801 Roeder Rd., Suite 900
Silver Spring, MD 20910
(800) 388-2227
Web site: www.nfcc.org

The NFCC is the nation's largest nonprofit credit counseling network. The NFCC offers help in finding credit, bankruptcy, and housing counselors, provides consumers with financial education, including budget worksheets and online debt calculators, and hosts national financial education initiatives such as the National Financial Literacy Poster Contest. NFCC publishes literature on financial issues including *Better Fortunes* and *More than One Way Out.*

United States Society for Ecological Economics (USSEE)
USSEE Secretariat Office, Association-Management Resources
PO Box 44326
West Allis, WI 53214
(800) 970-8438
e-mail: secretariat@ussee.org
Web site: www.ussee.org/v2/

USSEE is the U.S. branch of the International Society for Ecological Economics (ISEE), an association of academics and practitioners from a variety of fields who work together to advance "practical solutions toward an ecologically sustainable and economically viable future." The group works to shape university curriculum, promote interdisciplinary collaboration, and encourage student involvement. USSEE publishes educational papers as well as the quarterly newsletter *USSEE Newsletter.*

U.S. PIRG
44 Winter St., 4th Floor
Boston, MA 02108
(617) 747-4370
e-mail: membershipservices@pirg.org
Web site: www.uspirg.org

U.S. PIRG is the federation of state Public Interest Research Groups (PIRGs). The group advocates for the public on a variety of issues, including consumer protection, reforming health care, budget policy, and financial security. U.S. PIRG publishes the newsletter *U.S. PIRG Citizen Agenda.*

For Further Reading

Books

Epping, Randy Charles. *The 21st Century Economy—a Beginner's Guide.* New York: Vintage, 2009. Epping explains the world economy for beginners, including subprime mortgages, trade deficits, and macroeconomics.

Forbes, Steve, and Elizabeth Ames. *How Capitalism Will Save Us: Why Free People and Free Markets Are the Best Answer in Today's Economy.* New York: Crown Business, 2009. Forbes and Ames describe capitalism as the world's greatest economic system because it inspires innovation, creates abundance, and provides people with the opportunity to better their lives.

Graaf, John de, David Wann, and Thomas H. Naylor. *Affluenza.* San Francisco: Brett-Koehler, 2005. The authors describe affluenza, a "disease" of overconsumption and the constant need to acquire more things. They list the problems with this lifestyle, including bankruptcies, high levels of stress, and harm to the environment.

Jones, Van. *The Green Collar Economy: How One Solution Can Fix Our Two Biggest Problems.* New York: HarperOne, 2008. Jones explains how investing in environmentally friendly solutions will help level out socioeconomic inequality and avert environmental catastrophe.

Mitchell, Stacy. *Big-Box Swindle: The True Cost of Mega-Retailers and the Fight for America's Independent Businesses.* Boston: Beacon-Press, 2007. Mitchell details how huge retail chains have changed the face of business and, in the process, taken over large swatches of real estate, created sprawl, and hurt independent businesses.

Orman, Suze. *2009 Action Plan: Keeping Your Money Safe & Sound.* New York: Spiegel & Grau, 2008. The well-known financial adviser offers money advice. Topics include credit, retirement investing, saving, and spending.

Participant Media and Karl Weber. *Food Inc.: A Participant Guide: How Industrial Food Is Making Us Sicker, Fatter, and Poorer—and*

What You Can Do About It. New York: PublicAffairs, 2009. Experts in the field including Eric Schlosser and Michael Pollan provide essays on the hidden costs of cheap, industrialized food.

Posner, Richard A. *A Failure of Capitalism: The Crisis of '08 nd the Descent into Depression.* Cambridge, MA: Harvard University Press, 2009. Posner describes the factors that led to the economic crisis that began in 2008.

Shell, Ellen Ruppel. *Cheap: The High Cost of Discount Culture.* New York. Shell details the wide-ranging effects that the quest for cheap goods have had on the world, including lower wages, environmental degradation, and poor-quality merchandise.

Weber, Lauren. *In CHEAP We Trust: The Story of a Misunderstood American Virtue.* New York: Little, Brown, 2009. Weber traces the history of thrift in the United States and looks at present-day attitudes toward savings and thrift.

Periodicals

Berliner, Uri. "Hunkering Down in a Recession: A Return to Thrift?" NPR.org, March 11, 2009. www.npr.org/templates/story/story.php?storyId=101627769.

Carter, Majora. "Commentary: Green Way to Create Jobs, Save Cities," CNN.com, April 22, 2009. www.cnn.com/2009/TECH/science/04/22/carter.environment/index.html.

Crudele, John. "Personal Savings Rate Rise=Voodoo Economics," *New York Post*, July 2, 2009. www.nypost.com/p/news/business/item_XWNwiliVG6u9kUvOPteeiM;jsessionid=067422500CC0720B62DC9D067AD4AF03.

Crutsinger, Martin. "Americans Saving More When Economy Needs Spending Most," *Huffington Post*, February 1, 2009. www.huffingtonpost.com/2009/02/02/americans-saving-more-whe_n_163057.html.

Cruz, Humberto. "No Law Can Substitute for Credit Discipline," *Los Angeles Times*, September 13, 2009. http://articles.latimes.com/2009/sep/13/business/fi-credit-discipline13.

DeLong, Brad. "How Spending Stimulates," *The Week*, February 25, 2009. www.theweek.com/article/index/93614/How_spending_stimulates.

Ewing, Walter. "Immigrants Are Not a Fiscal Drain," *Sacramento Bee*, June 28, 2009. www.sacbee.com/325/story/1981220.html.

Friedman, Thomas L. "Adults Only, Please," *New York Times*, January 26, 2010. www.nytimes.com/2010/01/27/opinion/27friedman .html.

Gruber, Jonathan. "Universal Health Insurance Coverage or Economic Relief—a False Choice," *New England Journal of Medicine*, January 29, 2009. http://content.nejm.org/cgi/content/full/360/5/437.

Hanan, Stephen Mo. "Why Save Capitalism?" *Huffington Post*, December 7, 2008. www.huffingtonpost.com/stephen-mo-hanan/ why-save-capitalism_b_148914.html.

Keenan, Linda. "Home Values Plummeting. Economy in Meltdown. Blame?—Look in the Mirror!" Burbia.com, January 21, 2008. www.burbia.com/node/1574.

Kersten, Katherine. "Wal-Mart Confounds Its Critics," *Minneapolis Star-Tribune*, July 14, 2008. http://kerstenblog.startribune.com/ kerstenblog/?p=467.

Kostigen, Thomas. "The Green-Collar Jobs Myth," *MarketWatch*, June 19, 2009. www.marketwatch.com/story/the-green-collar-jobs-myth.

Krugman, Paul. "How Did Economists Get It So Wrong?" *New York Times*, September 2, 2009. www.nytimes.com/2009/09/06/ magazine/06Economic-t.htmlI?_r=1.

Leamer, Edward E. "Is Obama's Stimulus Working?" *Los Angeles Times*, August 19, 2009. www.latimes.com/news/opinion/opinionla/ la-oew-leamer-delong19-2009aug19,0,5376420.story.

Manning, Robert D. "Five Myths About America's Credit Card Debt," *Washington Post*, January 31, 2010. www.washingtonpostI .com/wp-dyn/content/article/2010/01/29/AR2010012902504I .htmlI?wprss=rss_print/outlook.

Merk, Axel. "Live Free or Die: Capitalism at Risk," *Financial Sense University*, January 13, 2009. www.financialsense.com/fsu/editorials/ merk/2009/0113.html.

Shlaes, Amity. "How to Make a Weak Economy Worse," *Wall Street Journal*, February 1, 2010. http://online.wsj.com/article/SB1000 142405274870380890457502498111091808.html.

Thaler, Richard. "It Doesn't Have to Hurt," *Newsweek*, April 11, 2009. www.newsweek.com/id/193476.

Washington Post Editorial Staff. "Is Capitalism Dead?" *Washington Post*, October 20, 2008. www.washingtonpost.com/wp-dyn/content/article/2008/10/19/AR2008101901416.html.

Web Sites

Bureau of Economic Analysis (BEA) (www.bea.gov). The Web site from the U.S. Department of Commerce offers publications, news, and statistics on the U.S. and global economies.

Dollars and Sense: Real World Economics (www.dollarsandsense.org/index.html). The *Dollars and Sense* Web site features articles and commentary about the economy, economic justice issues, and the media's coverage of economic issues.

MSN Money (http://moneycentral.msn.com/home.asp). MSN Money offers basic tutorials on money topics like banking, debt, and bankruptcy, as well as up-to-date articles on all aspects of the financial world.

Recovery.gov (www.recovery.gov/Pages/home.aspx). The U.S. Government official Web site for tracking the Recovery Act. The site features maps, charts, and graphs detailing how recovery funds are spent, provides help in finding recovery jobs, and offers extensive statistics on all aspects of the Recovery Act.

SmartMoney (www.Smartmoney.com). SmartMoney features articles on spending, investing, and other financial matters, plus financial planning tools.

U.S. Debt Clock.org (www.usdebtclock.org). U.S. Debt Clock.org offers a fascinating overview of the U.S. economy. The site features a host of real-time debt clocks showing dollar amounts of many economic indicators including the national debt, tax revenues collected, personal debt, and many more.

Young Money (www.youngmoney.com). The Web site for Young Money, a national organization specializing in personal finance education for young people, offers information on various aspects of money management, including financial aid, credit, debt, and careers.

Index

Singapore, 118
Socialism, 124–125
South Korea, 118
Spending. *See* Consumer spending;
    Deficit spending; Government
    spending
State Children's Health Insurance
    Program (S-CHIP), 33, 41–42
States, health care costs burdening,
    33–34
Stimulus plan
    is good for U.S. economy, 11–15
    is not good for U.S. economy,
        16–20
    targets for money from, 18
Structural adjustment programs,
    47–48

T
Taiwan, 118
Target, 66

U
Undocumented immigrants. *See*
    Illegal immigrants; Immigrant
    legalization
Uninsured Americans, 32
Union shops, 58
U.S. consumers
    buying power of, 7
    spending by, 8–9, 41
U.S. debt, 7–8, 26–29
U.S. dollar, 8
U.S. economy
    credit card reform is good for,
        103–106
    deficit spending will paralyze,
        25–29

discount retailers are good for,
    57–63
discount retailers harm, 64–69
green jobs are bad for, 98–102
green jobs are future of, 93–97
health care reform will grow,
    30–36
health care reform will not help,
    37–43
immigrant legalization would
    benefit, 70–75
immigrant legalization would
    not benefit, 76–81
impact of, on world economy, 7
stimulus plan is good for,
    11–15
stimulus plan is not good for,
    16–20
U.S. securities, 7–8

V
Visa programs, 80–81

W
Wages, at Walmart, 61, 62, 66
Walmart
    harms economy, 64–69
    is good for economy, 57–63
    workers at, 61, 62, 66–68
Water, Alice, *53*, 54
Weber, Christopher, 93–97
Wise, Timothy A., 45–50
World Bank, 46–47,
    116–117
World economy, 7, 117–118

Z
Zuckerman, Mort, 25–29

Picture Credits

AP Images, 13, 19, 53, 60, 80, 106, 119

Robyn Beck/AFP/Getty Images, 66

Kevin Dietsch/UPI/Landov, 82

Scott J. Ferrell/Congressional Quarterly/Getty Images, 28

Image copyright © Andrei Merkulov, 2010. Used under license from Shutterstock.com, 97

Image copyright © Andresr, 2010. Used under license from Shutterstock.com, 85

Image copyright © Joe Belanger, 2010. Used under license from Shutterstockcom, 10

Image copyright © TheGame, 2010. Used under license from Shutterstockcom, 44

Image copyright © Walter Keith Rice, 2010. Used under license from Shutterstock.com, 99

Image copyright ©Yuri Arcurs, 2010. Used under license from Shutterstock.com, 109

Saul Loeb/AFP/Getty Images, 42

David McNew/Getty Images, 32

Adrian Sanchez-Gonzalez/Landov, 72

Liu Xin/Xinhua/Landov, 126

Steve Zmina, 14, 18, 27, 35, 39, 47, 55, 59, 67, 78, 87, 95, 105, 110, 115